BATAK BLOOD
and
PROTESTANT SOUL

BATAK BLOOD
and
PROTESTANT SOUL

*The Development of National Batak Churches
in North Sumatra*

by

PAUL BODHOLDT PEDERSEN

WILLIAM B. EERDMANS PUBLISHING COMPANY
GRAND RAPIDS, MICHIGAN

Copyright © 1970 by Wm. B. Eerdmans Publishing Co.
All rights reserved
Library of Congress Catalog Card Number: 71-80876
Printed in the United States of America

279.1
P37
c.2

To
RADJA PONTAS LUMBANTOBING
who had the courage and prophetic insight
to guide the Batak people toward the gospel

36009

EDITORIAL FOREWORD

Christian World Mission Books have been projected as a library of paperback volumes on every aspect of the world mission of the church of Christ — history, theory, methods, functional concerns, regional studies, biography, and also source material long unavailable to students. One purpose is to make available to general historians and the growing number of readers factual information about mission, since they are now discovering its importance in international relations and cultural interchange. The books are also intended to be tools for teachers and students of world mission and church history, but are equally directed to pastors and laymen in the churches. Sound scholarship underlies these books, but they are not directed primarily toward the technical scholar and expert. Although intended primarily for the North American public, it is hoped that these books will receive wide international use. The authors have been recruited from many nations and churches, including a wide range of Protestants, Roman Catholics, and hopefully Orthodox eventually. May these books contribute to dialogue on the fundamentals of mission in the highly creative period just opening.

The present volume appears in the series "Mission Studies." It is directed toward filling the long-standing gap in English literature on the Batak churches of Sumatra, and it will correct many popular misconceptions of those churches current in the West as well as offer an historical overview of their development and a sympathetic interpretation of their present circumstances. Paul B. Pedersen became acquainted with the Batak Christians and began his research while serving as chaplain at Nommensen University at Medan and Siantar under appointment by the Lutheran World Federation.

R. Pierce Beaver
Editor

CONTENTS

PREFACE

A STUDY OF THE TRANSITIONAL STAGES LEADING UP TO independent Batak churches will help us estimate the past contribution of foreign missionary organizations, understand the rapidly changing present context in Indonesia, and anticipate problems of national churches emerging from the mission field. As these Batak churches become less dependent on missionary-sending Western churches they are developing their own application of Christian theology to the Indonesian national context. The destination of these transitional changes is uncertain, but the direction of change can be studied by examining the development from traditional religion to mission field and from mission field to independent national churches. The eclectic product of transitional change borrows both from indigenous and foreign sources of influence as modernization becomes disassociated from Westernization.

The Christian Bataks are a unique people with a vivid awareness of their identity both as Bataks and as Christians. In the process of change religion has been closely associated with Batak culture and society. The plurality of Batak churches reflects a wide divergence of approaches used by missionary organizations to introduce Christianity and a variety of responses by Bataks to those different strategies. The willingness of the Bataks to accept new influences has led them into modern ideologies, prosperous coastal regions, and the Christian faith often more rapidly and in larger numbers than these ideologies, regions, and churches were able to receive them.

In the hope that the reader will be stimulated to explore the Batak culture and religion in greater depth, the sources used have been liberally footnoted. While many better-known German and Dutch sources have been neglected, other English and Indonesian sources have been introduced to the reader which would be otherwise inaccessible. Unless otherwise indicated, the translations from Indonesian have been made by myself. For translations from the German and the Dutch I acknowledge the assistance of Dr. Rolf Knierim and Dr. Hans Ruyter respectively, both members of the Claremont Graduate School faculty, Claremont, California.

In the text of this study unordained national workers will be referred to as "teachers" or "evangelists," while ordained national workers in the churches will be referred to as "pendeta." Personnel of foreign missionary organizations will be referred to as "missionaries." While I have used the modern Indonesian spelling throughout, some Indonesian names and numerous direct quotations have retained the Dutch spelling of Indonesian terms. Other irregularities include the spelling of "Batak," which was once spelled "Batta," and the references to "Batavia," now known as "Djakarta," the capital city of Indonesia. Where the original Batak or Indonesian term is retained, an English approximation is included in parentheses and the term is italicized when first introduced.

Four aids are included to clarify the many names of churches and locations in Batakland. The first of these is a list of abbreviations for organizational names used in the study (p. 13). Second, there is a map locating the places mentioned (p. 16). Third, there is a chart comparing the growth in membership of the various Batak churches (p. 203). Fourth, there is a list of Protestant church organizations in North Sumatra registered with the Department of Religion (p. 201).

A number of libraries were particularly helpful in supplying materials for research. M. H. Harrison of the Missionary Research Library; Helen M. Knubel of the Lutheran Council in the USA Office of Research, Statistics, and Archives; Mrs. Elsie Lund from the library of the Board of Missions of the Methodist Church; and the Oegstgeest Bibliotheek Nederlandse Zendingshogeschool were particularly helpful. Dr. William Liddle, Rev. Howard Gering, H. Neumann, Fr. Guido Tharappel, Mrs. H. L. Tobing, and other friends in

Indonesia supplied much valuable material. Dr. Lothar Schreiner, Dr. R. Pierce Beaver, and especially Rev. Edward Nyhus provided valuable advice as the study progressed. Rev. Nyhus, Professor of Church History at Nommensen Seminary, circulated a draft of this study among church leaders in North Sumatra soliciting valuable suggestions from Ephorus J. Sitorus and Secretary General W. Lumbantobing of the HKI, Pendeta Petrus Purba from the GKPS, Rev. Fr. Linus Fäh, O.F.M., Cap from the Roman Catholic Seminary at Pematang Siantar, Missionary Werner Grothaus, working with the GBKP, and others. My wife Joanne, Mrs. David Eichner and Evonne Domyahn were helpful in proofreading the manuscript. Many others have provided valuable encouragement along the way. While I am indebted to all these people, I assume full responsibility for the opinions expressed in the study.

This survey explores selected Batak churches and their problems according to available materials. I can only hope the reader enjoys reading the material as much as I have enjoyed writing it.

PAUL PEDERSEN

LIST OF ABBREVIATIONS

ABCFM	American Board of Commissioners for Foreign Missions
BNZ	Batak Nias Zending (Batak Nias Mission)
CYCOM	Commission on Younger Churches and Orphaned Missions
DGI	Dewan Geredja-Geredja di Indonesia (Indonesian Council of Churches)
FKIP	Fakultas Keguruan dan Ilmu Pendidikan (Department of Education and Teacher Training)
GBKP	Geredja Batak Karo Protestant (Karo Protestant Church)
GKPI	Geredja Kristen Protestant Indonesia (Indonesian Protestant Christian Church)
GKPS	Geredja Kristen Protestant Simalungun (Simalungun Protestant Christian Church)
GMKI	Gerakan Mahasiswa Kristen Indonesia (Indonesian Christian Student Movement)
HChB	Huria Christen Batak (Batak Christian Church)
HKB	Hatopan Kristen Batak (Batak Christian Federation)
HKBP	Huria Kristen Batak Protestant (Batak Protestant Christian Church)
HKI	Huria Kristen Indonesia (Indonesian Christian Church)
IMC	International Missionary Council
LWF	Lutheran World Federation
NKPS	Namaposo Kristen Protestant Simalungun (Simalungun Protestant Christian Youth)
NLC	National Lutheran Council
NZG	Nederlands Zendingsgenootschap

OMF	Overseas Missionary Fellowship
PKB	Perhimpunan Kristen Batak (Batak Christian Church)
PKI	Parti Komunist Indonesia (Indonesian Communist Party)
PRRI	Pemerintah Revolusioner Republik Indonesia (Revolutionary Government of the Republic of Indonesia)
PSK	Paguruan Saksi ni Kristus (Witnesses for Christ)
RMG	Rheinischen Mission
SCM	Student Christian Movement
SGI	Sekolah Guru Indjil (Bible Teachers' School)
STT	Sekolah Tinggi Theologia (School of Theology)
TOBA	Tabahen Oeang Bahen Arta (Money for Social Welfare)
WCC	World Council of Churches
YMCA	Young Men's Christian Association

BATAK BLOOD
and
PROTESTANT SOUL

I

BATAK SOCIETY AND RELIGION

1. Foreign Influences

For many years the Batak tribes of North Sumatra were isolated from other Indonesian or foreign contacts by the mountainous geography of the region and their own self-imposed isolation. Although relatively secluded from the dominant cultures and religions of Southeast Asia, the Bataks had developed their own complex social, legal, and religious systems. It was thus necessary to adapt Christian concepts to the vocabulary and social structure of traditional Batak society. Batak culture had already demonstrated its strength by accommodating and absorbing other foreign influences into traditional Batak culture. The problem for missionaries was how to introduce Christianity without, on the one hand, seriously weakening Batak society or, on the other hand, being absorbed into traditional Batak culture.

While the Bataks had borrowed from Hindu and Buddhist cultures surrounding Batakland, neither religion had dominated Batak society. The devout and dynamic Muslims of Atjeh to the North and Minangkabau to the South had also failed to displace traditional Batak beliefs. Other Indonesian and Western observers as far back as Marco Polo had characterized the Bataks as a fierce, cannibalistic people to be avoided by

17

all outsiders. William Marsden, in his *History of Sumatra,* was the first to recognize that the Bataks actually had a highly developed civilization with social, legal, and religious sophistication.[1]

For most Bataks their first contact with Western civilization was through Christian missionaries. The Governor of Portuguese Malacca had tried to solicit Batak support against Atjehnese assaults of 1537-1551 without success. The Dutch East Indies Company secured a trade agreement with several Batak *radjas* (tribal chiefs) as early as 1694, but, although a Dutch representative was stationed on the west coast of Sumatra, they succeeded in penetrating only the coastal fringe of Batakland. The British established trading posts at Tapian Na Uli on the Bay of Sibolga between 1725 and 1824 to provide salt and fresh water for ships going to Calcutta. The English claimed that the "Tapian Na Uli Territories" as far into Batakland as the second of three ranges of hills dividing Sumatra were under British rule. This was done largely to prevent other European powers from making a claim in the area, and the Bataks were themselves unaware that they were "British subjects."[2]

The Batak culture can be traced back to a series of migrations from South China, Yünnan, and North Viet Nam sometime during the eighth and seventh centuries B.C.[3] The early Bataks, settling in the region of Lake Toba in North Sumatra, were probably shifting cultivators of root crops or perhaps rice with a nonmetallic technology. Their religion, judging from similarities with other Proto Malay cultures, involved a respect for the powers of nature and the firm belief that ancestral spirits took a lively interest in the behavior of their descendants.

---

[1] William Marsden, *The History of Sumatra,* p. 301. Also note Edwin M. Loeb, *Sumatra, Its History and People,* pp. 20ff.

[2] Benjamin Heyne, *Tracts, Historical and Statistical on India; An Account of Sumatra* (London: Black, Perry, 1814), p. 375. Also note Mangaradja Onggang Parlindungan, *Tuanku Rao* (Djakarta: Penerbit Tandjung Pengharapan, 1964), pp. 625ff.

[3] Robert von Heine-Geldern, "Prehistoric Research in the Netherlands Indies," in *Science and Scientists in the Netherlands Indies,* pp. 147f.

As the Bataks prospered they were differentiated from two exogamous patrilineal units into tribal groups of Toba, Pak-Pak, Karo, Simalungun, Angkola, and Mandailing Bataks. Others include the Alas, Gayo, and Sim-Sim tribal groups as part of the Batak people. A separate grouping of Bataks in the Asahan River valley called Pardembanan were probably a later migration from the Toba region. Each tribal group recognized a cousin-relationship with the other Batak tribes but developed independent variations of culture and custom. The Toba Batak language and culture is generally considered nearest to the original root form of Batak traditions. The emphasis of this first chapter shall be on the Toba Batak traditional religion and social organization.

Sometime after 2000 B.C. and before A.D. 1500 the Batak culture was influenced by a Hindu-Buddhist civilization in the southern and coastal regions of North Sumatra. Foreign colonization may have come directly from India or possibly from Java but most likely from the Minangkabau Malays of West-Central Sumatra. Dozens of abandoned temples and ruins in the Asahan valley and southern Batakland testify to a highly developed civilization in the twelfth and thirteenth centuries. When Islam entered Indonesia through Sumatra, in the thirteenth and fourteenth centuries, Hindu-Javanese contact was cut off, isolating the Bataks and causing the remaining foreigners and their culture to be assimilated into the indigenous population.[4]

By this time the Bataks had developed a distinctive culture with a written religious liturgy, medico-religious practitioners, elaborate local leadership patterns, a kin-based class system, sophisticated irrigation engineering, an authoritative legal code, and sciences of medical, astronomical, and mathematical

---

4 Loeb, *op. cit.,* pp. 20f. Also note F. M. Schnitger, *The Archeology of Hindoo Sumatra* (Leiden: E. J. Brill, 1937), p. 37; Robert von Heine-Geldern, "The Archeology and Art of Sumatra," in Loeb, *op. cit.,* pp. 305-31; H. H. Bartlett, "The Symbolic Grave-Post (Anisan) of the Batak of Asahan," *Papers of the Michigan Academy of Science, Arts and Letters,* I, 2; H. H. Bartlett, "A Batak and Malay Chant on Rice Cultivation, with Introductory Notes on Bilingualism and Acculturation in Indonesia," *Proceedings of the American Philosophical Society,* XCVI (1952), 629-52.

knowledge. Their written language and barkbook literature borrowed heavily from Sanskrit vocabulary and style of writing. The introduction of wet-rice agriculture, the horse, the plow, style of dwelling, chess, cotton, and the spinning wheel indicates the breadth of influence throughout society, while the incorporation of foreign terminology into their religious cosmology indicates its depth.

The Bataks were never under direct foreign rule as dependent colonies during this time. Dr. Philip Tobing points out several factors limiting foreign influence. The Hindu-Javanese contacts were largely restricted to the coastal areas and borderlands of the Batak-inhabited area. These contacts were largely in the economic sphere, inadequate to transmit a more refined culture from one society to another. The Toba Bataks were conservative by nature, accepting foreign elements only when they could be accommodated by traditional cosmology.[5]

2. TRADITIONAL RELIGIOUS BELIEFS

When Christian missionaries arrived among the Bataks they found them to be a devoutly zealous people with a vivid awareness of religious power in the world around them. While many of these religious notions were condemned by the missionaries, Batak piety toward the dynamic activity of religious power was preserved in a Christian context. The missionaries found it convenient if not essential to explain their message in traditional terms.

Traditional Batak cosmology divided existence into three levels or worlds. The upper world was the realm of the High God, Mula Djadi Na Bolon, and the spirits of departed ancestors. The middle world was the arena of human activity; and the under world was the home of ghosts and demons, ruled by Naga Padoha the serpent. The gods were thought to live like men with their wives and children, slaves and cattle, playing, waging war, and arguing among themselves. There are legends telling how men once found their way from earth to

---

[5] Philip L. Tobing, *The Structure of the Toba Batak Belief in the High God*, pp. 18-19.

the upper world and met with the High God. This was before human pride destroyed the path to the upper world. Other stories tell how daughters of the gods descended to earth and married humans. The Batak was not intimidated by his gods and would occasionally attempt to deceive them, sacrificing an egg and declaring it to be a white buffalo, curse them when things went wrong, and once the Bataks were said to have declared war against their gods and bombarded them from a mountaintop![6]

The Toba Batak experienced all cosmic space as a totality of under world, upper world, and middle world in which each layer had a special function in the harmony of existence. Disruption of this harmony would mean the annihilation of the whole cosmos. Batak mythology described a tree of life, reaching from the under world to the upper world, symbolic of the High God in uniting all existence and representing the totality of cosmic order. The fate of every man was recorded on this tree of life from which all life originated.

The Batak organization of time also suggests a unified world view, with each twenty-four-hour day and twelve-month year viewed as a totality. Each month was associated with a part of the High God's body, the fifth and eighth months being his blood. The Toba Batak did not emphasize quantitatively measurable time but experienced every space of time qualitatively and concretely. Special days were set aside for building a house, fighting a war, or getting married as either favorable, indifferent, or unfavorable. The day itself possessed power of holiness, bliss, and doom. Each day was evaluated through a *porhalaan,* calendar-type oracle instrument, which is still sometimes consulted by modern Bataks.

Space was viewed as neither homogeneous nor neutral but with substance. Each point of the compass had its value, with power to affect the life and prosperity of men. The value of each point on the compass varied according to the time of the year, implying that the substance of space and its power were determined by time. The course of time could only be

---

6 Loeb, *op. cit.,* p. 75. Also note Johannes Warneck, *The Living Christ and Dying Heathenism,* p. 38.

determined through changes in space without which there would be no notion of time. Time and space formed an essential unity in their cosmic view.

There was no clear distinction between representation and identity in Batak religious thought, and the symbol participated in the reality it represented. Natural objects or carved god-representations possessed symbolic power and could even be punished if not sufficiently efficacious. All reality was tied together in a single identity. "Life and death, oneness and multiplicity, good, half-heartedness and evil, etc., are not absolute but relative contrasts, which presuppose and generate each other. Their unity reconciles them."[7]

Johannes Warneck suggests that the idea of a High God in Batak religion had degenerated from an original monotheism, resembling the Judaeo-Christian idea of God, to a *deus otiosus* having withdrawn to the upper world.[8] In his place a *debata na tolu* or *Trimurti* notion of three gods was popularized in the deities Batara Guru, Soripada, and Mangalabulan. Even these three gods had little direct communication with men except through myths and ritual prayers. According to one tradition Batara Guru was called down to men once but declared the problems of the middle world were too difficult and that in the future he should be left in peace.

Rejecting the description of the High God as deus otiosus, Dr. Philip Tobing introduces the notion of an underlying, naturalistic-monistic trend, which he calls totalitarian religious thinking, to describe traditional Batak religion.[9] The Batak did not distinguish between different powers and aspects of the High God because they experienced each part as a totality, each microcosm as a macrocosm. This synthetic-concrete approach contrasts sharply with the analytic-categorical approach of Western scientific thought. The High God is not only a deus otiosus but also a dynamic incorporation of all creation, good and evil, multiplicity and oneness. He is the creator-god who "flattens the skull, twines the bowels,

[7] Tobing, *op. cit.*, p. 21.
[8] *Ibid.*, p. 23.
[9] *Ibid.*, p. 21.

sets agoing the heart, expands the liver, opens the mouth, makes clear the eyes of the sons of men."[10]

Belief in the High God was belief in a world order, excluding arbitrariness and identifying god and community. The High God not only created the cosmos but was himself the cosmos and man the microcosmos. Every Toba Batak considered himself a manifestation of the High God and the *adat* (customary law), which guided the individual and the community and guarded the microcosmic reflection of macrocosmic order. "The adat, which must be the guide in every situation, is the microcosmic order. The Tobanese and his community must observe the adat on penalty of disasters, such as epidemics, famine, etc...."[11]

The whole personal and social life of the Batak was permeated with religious meaning, guided by religious motives, and dominated by supernatural concepts through the gods, ancestors, and dynamic cosmos in which he lived. In his personal and social life the religious element was basic to all practices and activities. Being surrounded by potentially dangerous forces it was natural for the Batak to seek magicoreligious means of augmenting his power.

The early missionaries frequently commented that mixed motives of both fear and love attracted, impressed, and won the Bataks over to Christianity. "The ruthless person makes a strong impression because the heathen thinks that he would not make so bold without power to correspond at his command."[12] The Bataks have a saying that man comes to earth to eat rice. In his quest for nourishment and well-being the Batak was not attracted but repelled by the supernatural and avoided contact with those powers except to protect his own well-being. The missionaries understood this as a basic materialistic anxiety for preservation of earthly goods and exploitation of religious power for private advantage, prosperity, or prestige. The early missionaries identified the central religious attitude as a feeling of dependence on sinister powers,

---

10 Warneck, *op. cit.*, p. 29.

11 Tobing, *op. cit.*, pp. 132-33.

12 Gottfried Simon, *The Progress and Arrest of Islam in Sumatra*, p. 14.

spirits, and the fear of the unknown. "It is fear of these powers which alone impels those heathen to seek ways and means of averting their pernicious influence."[13] The gods, however, were considered apathetic spectators, observing human conflict from far in the background. Even the High God was sometimes characterized as "an old weak grandfather, who always excuses the faults of his grandchildren."[14]

The Batak's conception of virtue and merit was sometimes diametrically opposed to the Judaeo-Christian ethic. He considered bravery essential for entrance into the kingdom of the dead. As a token of this bravery the guardian of souls would be likely to ask him how many heads he had taken. An essential provision for posterity was the continuation of his family. To remain unmarried or, in regions where sexual intercourse between unmarried persons was no disgrace, to practice continence was a serious violation. The ethical paradox was that "the murderer finds entrance to the spirit world, whereas the man he murders does not, because he stands condemned by the judgment of God; and the immoral person, because he has fulfilled his sexual obligations, is accepted whereas the chaste person is rejected."[15] In like manner the warrior who died in battle could not enter the kingdom of the dead because his death proved supernatural judgment against him, while another who fled the battlefield out of cowardice was justified by the gods. The leper deserved to have his house burned down around him since terrible disease was a clear sign of divine judgment.

Religion for the Toba Batak was acceptance of a higher reality as the object of his fear and worship on which he could depend as a powerful and resourceful ally. This religious view ignored any moral criterion or principle, such as man's responsibility to God or love for his neighbor, in favor of self-preservation, recognizing the community as an extension of the self. While his life was permeated with religious motives this was actually a means of self-preservation through

13 Warneck, *op. cit.*, p. 27.

14 *Ibid.*, p. 252.

15 Simon, *op. cit.*, p. 103.

which the Batak would "assert himself with his helplessness and craftiness, with his vitality and his naïve self-preservation, in the midst of a world which he does not understand and which overwhelms him threatening his elementary and vital desires."[16]

It was the power, or promise of power, which first attracted the Batak to Christianity. The fear and worship of God stood beyond any moral criterion, and to follow him was to share in his superiority, power, and prestige. For the early Batak Christians "faith could be characterized as conscript labour of the intellect carried out as a matter of course."[17]

Self-preservation for the individual and for the community demanded power. Egoism became self-justifying and it was preferable to exploit power, even divine power, than to obey it. Hendrik Kraemer chooses the Batak word *hasanga-pon* (highness, prestige) as a key concept to understanding Batak religious attitudes. "Hence, his strong self-assertion, his comparative imperviability to a sense of personal guilt or shortcoming, his abhorrence of the thought of being or being made *malu* (embarrassed)."[18] There was a desire among the Bataks not only to serve God but to possess him. Christianity, in its emphasis on success as a sign of God's goodwill, failed to eliminate that desire. "If an undertaking has been successful, it means that it must have been the will of God. If a marriage is childless, then God cannot have willed it, and the couple must be divorced."[19]

The spirit-peopled world of the Toba Batak was designed around his special concern for his own personified *tondi*, which has been translated to mean "soul-stuff." The descriptions of the tondi give it qualities of a material object, although formless as air. While the tondi is not simply a human quality, there is a distinction made between the static condition of the body and the dynamic mobility embodied in

---

[16] Hendrik Kraemer, *From Mission Field to Independent Church*, p. 51. Also note Simon, *op. cit.*, p. 176.

[17] Kraemer, *op. cit.*, p. 54.

[18] *Ibid.*, p. 53.

[19] Julia Sarumpaet-Hutabarat, "Women Under the Adat," *Lutheran World*, II (Summer, 1955), p. 121.

the tondi. The tondi as a whole dwells in all parts of the body, but the tondi and person are integral to each other and not separate entities. All experiences are ascribed to the activity of one's tondi much as we attribute behavior to an individual's personality. When represented as life-stuff the tondi is also present in animals and plants, but not as abundantly as in humans. Nearly every object of nature was thought to have a prescribed quantity of animating tondi that could be brought into focus by special circumstances.

The tondi was considered to have an independent existence and the ability to exert influence on present and future happenings. The tondi of living men, of the deceased, and of those still to come was with the High God in the upper world and associated with him in such a way that through the tondi the High God himself was in all men and beings. The entire religious life of the Batak, seeking his welfare in this world and the next, was fulfilled through nursing his own tondi according to its sometimes fickle whims.

The tondi determined each man's fate. Before birth each man's tondi would ask for a leaf from the tree of life on which would be written his destiny. The tondi was free to choose whichever role in life it wished, and the Batak calls his destiny "that which his tondi has asked for."[20] If things went well for a Batak he would credit his tondi for having made a good choice, and if things went badly he would blame his tondi. The wishes of the person need not agree with those of his tondi; but it was the will of the tondi, not the person, which would prevail. The Batak might react defiantly against his tondi but would usually be submissive, adopting a fatalistic attitude and calm resignation to whatever happened. Both gods and men were bound by the lot that one's tondi had chosen. The tondi could be enticed to wander from the body by magical acts against the person, or it could be displaced by evil spirits. If it wandered or became sufficiently weak, the individual would become ill and die. To remain well and strong it was good practice to make an occasional offering to

[20] H. G. Quaritch Wales, "The Cosmological Aspect of Indonesian Religion," *Journal of the Royal Asiatic Society,* 1959, p. 129.

one's own tondi. When on good terms, one's tondi would warn him against harm, inspire him with courage in war, and become a valuable ally in his struggle against the cosmos.

The tondi was not the better self in man or even the spiritual side of his person. It would not punish a man or leave him for having done evil and, unlike a conscience, had little to do with moral judgments of right or wrong. It might, however, react unfavorably toward a man's failure to comply with established tradition. It was believed that the tondi would be asked by the High God if the person was able to acquire property, whether he begat children, and whether he was brave, judging each tondi according to values that prevail in the Batak's middle-world life.[21]

The tondi existed in every aspect of the person, including his hair, fingernails, sweat, tears, urine, excrement, shadow, and even in his name. Possession of a person's belongings could be a source of sympathetic magical power over his tondi. For that reason every piece of clothing, strand of hair, footprint, object on which his shadow had fallen, and even his name were carefully guarded. Bataks still refrain from revealing their first name and, in most cases, are known only by their sib-group surname.

The tondi demonstrated its strength in a man's wealth, descendants, fidelity in carrying on ancestral traditions, courage, and eloquence of expression. It was important that the tondi be kept strong and secure in the person, and the Batak greeting of *Horas!* (hard, strong, firm-fixed) expressed hope that the Batak's tondi be firmly fixed to him and kept strong. Another common salutation was "pir ma tondi mardingin, horas tondi matogu!" (may your tondi be firm and cool, may your tondi be firm and strong). Coolness promoted stability of a tondi, while heat, anger, or excitement were prejudicial to its welfare. A customary farewell is "horas be ma!" (may both of us be strong).[22]

The tondi had no strong allegiance to the person it in-

---

21 Warneck, *op. cit.*, p. 58.

22 J. C. Vergouwen, *The Social Organization and Customary Law of the Toba Batak of Northern Sumatra*, p. 81.

habited. It was a problem to keep the tondi and the person living together peacefully, for if the tondi disliked its environment it could be lured away. The tondi did not essentially belong to the person and might have little interest in maintaining its temporary dwelling. A person served his tondi by honoring it and feeding it well. Occasional celebrations called *mangupa* were held either as a mark of gratitude to a tondi that had undergone difficulty or as encouragement to withstand approaching danger. This consisted of eating a common meal together, appropriate speeches being made and presents being exchanged. Eating was an important ceremony in the Batak's life. His food was rich in tondi power and was eaten in peace and quiet without disturbance. The important thing in eating was not the food itself but the tondi power that the food contained. When food was sacrificed, the spirits would receive the tondi power and the worshipers only the material portion left over.[23] At feasts and festivals a meal was thought to bring one's tondi into a pleasant frame of mind so that blessings could be exchanged, problems resolved, important decisions made, harmony established, and a favorable atmosphere created. A meal was the appropriate ceremony preceding important decisions or judgments, and a means of thanksgiving after the aims of the meeting had been achieved.

The ceremony of cannibalism among the Toba Bataks was designed to secure and supplement tondi power through consuming human parts especially potent in tondi, such as the blood, heart, palms of hands, or soles of the feet. Cannibalism was appropriate punishment for adultery, midnight robbery, intramarriage within the clan, and treacherous attacks on house, village, or person during wars of importance between villages. On other occasions the victim volunteered to be eaten as a means of gaining status among his peers and immortality through the bodies of their descendants. If the victim was not a volunteer he had a regular trial and sentence was formally passed before public assembly in the presence of chiefs from neighboring villages. Either as a volunteer or a dangerous criminal, the victim represented a source of extraordinary

---

23 Warneck, *op. cit.*, p. 50.

power. "By eating an enemy one obtains his soul qualities; also by eating him one identifies oneself with him, and so renders him (his soul) powerless to work further damage."[24]

The spoken word could also convey power, bringing benediction or calamity. "Words can summon powers that bring ruin or good fortune. Bad words, invective, insulting words, or words which contain a malediction all stir up evil. And for almost no offense are there so many [Batak] terms as for verbal insult."[25] This was especially true for prayers and ritual addresses where the play of homonymous words, sounds, terms, and proverbs multiplied the efficacy of their power. "The Batak prayer is not a magical formula, nor is the sacrifice a magical ceremony. The gods and spirits are begged, not forced, by prayer."[26]

The symbols of authority themselves emanate power through their quality of *sahala*. Dr. Andar Lumbantobing equates the concept of sahala with that of *mana* in Melanesian and Polynesian ethnology. "A person who possesses authority, riches and offspring is one who possesses sahala. The sahala of a person increases as these things increase."[27] Vergouwen equates the Toba Batak idea of sahala with the acquisition of wealth, respect, and honor from which power can accrue, like the Western notion of success, in direct proportion to his courage, eloquence, and authority.[28] It was possible to secure sahala to replenish one's own supply since sahala would automatically flow from one object to another on contact. Possessions of powerful men were thought to emanate sahala.

When a man died his tondi left him, but remained a power in the middle world of ancestral spirits, who must be appeased through the proper observance of sacred rites and customs they instituted during life. The Batak family included both

---

24 Loeb, *op. cit.*, p. 93.

25 Vergouwen, *op. cit.*, p. 95.

26 Loeb, *op. cit.*, p. 93.

27 Andar Lumbantobing, "Sahala of a Medicine Man and a Theological Graduate," *South East Asian Journal of Theology*, January, 1963, p. 7; also Tobing, *op. cit.*, p. 93.

28 Vergouwen, *op. cit.*, p. 83.

living and dead, with the fortunes of the living dependent on the goodwill of the ancestors and the welfare of those ancestors dependent on homage and sacrifices by the living for their benefit.

The most powerful of the *begu* (ancestral spirits) were called *sombaon,* who in life had founded great communities and had at least seven generations of descendants. At feasts held in their honor the sombaon received the sacrifices of the entire community. The local sombaon was invoked at all important religious ceremonies as the most powerful spirit of the patrilineal community, held in as great esteem among the living as he was among the dead.

Warneck cites instances where a father or grandfather, neglected and abominably treated in his last years — since nothing was to be hoped or feared from him — would be honored with an elaborate funeral, many sacrifices, and testimonials to his heroism by prudent descendants.[29] The dead were half-friend and half-enemy, jealous of the living but entirely dependent on them for regular sacrifices since, should the memory of a dead ancestor be forgotten, he also would cease to exist.[30] Should a Batak die without descendants, no one would feel bound to serve and honor him after death.

The descendants, on the other hand, were assured that by sacrifices they could secure assistance from the ancestors and thereby avoid disaster, illness, and misfortune. The worship of ancestors was therefore based more on fear than piety and acted as a powerful conservative force in society. Irreverent behavior toward the spirits, such as innovation and departure from traditional customs, brought immediate supernatural judgment. The worst criticism of a Batak was that he had done something never done before and thereby violated tradition.[31] The judgment of the ancestors fell not only on the individual but on the whole community.

While the missionaries opposed the tondi-cult, much that was equally pagan in character and origin was not clearly

29 Warneck, *op. cit.,* pp. 64-65.
30 *Ibid.,* p. 63.
31 *Ibid.,* p. 152.

understood and therefore tolerated. These expressions of religious dynamism were either considered harmless customs, universal characteristics of humanity, or they were given a superficial Christian veneer that has obscured their pagan origin. The stories of miracles in the Scriptures often harmonized with traditional religious beliefs. The Bataks could easily understand that Samson's hair was his source of strength, that people were healed by napkins saturated with sweat from a saint, that a woman touched the hem of Christ's garment and was healed, that the sick were satisfied if Peter's shadow fell on them, or that spittle could heal blindness.

3. TRADITIONAL LEADERSHIP

Although there was no clear differentiation in traditional Batak society between religious and secular leadership, the *datu* functioned as a priest and the radja as village chief. Bartlett cites research on the use of the title datu throughout the Pacific islands in its various meanings as king, chief, or priest. In the more remote islands datu designates the highest chief or king, while in the islands nearer the old Hindu sphere of influence, the term refers to a priesthood, higher nobility, or a generally applicable title of respect.[32] This leads Bartlett to conclude that the office of datu was the supreme authority before Hindu influence, during which time the office of radja as secular ruler was introduced to divide the leadership responsibilities of society.

The function of the Batak datu, referred to as *hadatuon*, combines elements of magic with essentially religious medical and instructional tasks, which the datu referred to as *hordja* or labors. The ordinary man was dependent on expert religious knowledge and specialized talent to supplement his own power in the struggle with the cosmos. Although any adult Batak could make sacrifices to the spirits, the office of datu developed a highly specialized system of liturgy, worship-objects, and methods not known to the general public. The datu could entice the tondi of the living and the begu of the

---

32 H. H. Bartlett, "The Labors of the Datoe," *Papers of the Michigan Academy of Science, Arts and Letters, 1929-1930,* XII (1930), 6.

dead. He could propitiate and coerce unfriendly spirits through curative medicinal and magical formula. He could control the weather, influence the harvest, and ascertain the future. The datu functioned as a physician to treat the sick and protect the healthy through his acquaintance with the ways of tondi and begu. As a clairvoyant he set appropriate dates for declaring war, getting married, or building a house. He could also read the entrails of a chicken or small animal to interpret the meaning of past and present events, or predict the future.

As a mediator between man and the world of magic, everything concerning the datu was itself considered magical and was said to have much sahala or mana. He was highly respected as a source of life, well-being, happiness, and good fortune by those associated with him. He was always called upon to be present at important family events and consulted about decisions such as an appropriate time, appropriate name, selection of marriage partners, and funeral rites.[33]

In the magico-religious world of the Bataks, cleansing ceremonies and special rites were repeatedly necessary to protect the tondi from possible impurity or bad influences. Each ceremony demanded a sacrifice of some sort, and the liturgy was accompanied with precise ritual and ceremony. When sickness or disaster struck it was the function of the datu to discover the nature of the disturbance and restore the equilibrium of the microcosm. Since so much of the ritual was secretive, the office of datu was usually passed on to his son following an intensive initiation and instruction.

The datu had a collection of carved images and objects such as the *tunggal panaluan* staff to assist him. These objects were not themselves worshiped and had religious value only insofar as they were artificially supplied with tondi power through a potion of material known as *pupuk,* especially powerful in tondi power. The object became a symbolic representation of supernatural power known as *pagar* (fence) to protect persons, houses, or whole villages from evil spirits. As in the case of the tunggal panaluan staff there are elaborate

---

33 Warneck, *op. cit.,* p. 51.

legends associating the objects with powerful events, persons, or forces in the distant past.

Besides the datu there was a *Si-baso* or *shaman,* usually a woman, who served as spiritual medium between the Batak and his ancestral spirit. This person was selected by the spirits themselves, who displaced her own tondi and communicated directly with the community by speaking through the shaman. Because the shaman led a particularly difficult life and was required to observe many taboos, few persons wished to serve in this capacity.[34]

While the power of these religious leaders extended into the secular as well as sacred realms, the village chief or radja was the ultimate village authority. Each village chief was the personified adat. But he was also the personified community.[35] The soul of the chief could either exert a dreaded influence on his subjects or be a source of great happiness. "His power proves that he has much and strong soul stuff, and therefore can be dangerous. In a law court it is not so much the juridical authority as the soul of the judge that is feared."[36]

The rise or decline of rulers, their lineages, their prosperity, power, prestige, or influence was regarded as an indication of the presence or absence of special potency. The radja possessed *sahala haradjaon* (quality of power), the natural result of which was *sahala hasangapon* (quality of being respected). "They are the qualities which dwell in a chief and which, thanks to their existence, entitle him to respect, veneration and, as the bearer of authority, to docility and obedience."[37]

The orders promulgated by the radja must conform with the adat. They were deliberated by all adult men in the community and finally decided upon by a majority in the village council. While in some areas of Batakland the radja could be quite autocratic, he risked losing members of his

34 *Ibid.,* pp. 71-73.
35 Tobing, *op. cit.,* pp. 20ff.
36 Warneck, *op. cit.,* p. 53.
37 Vergouwen, *op. cit.,* p. 131.

community to neighboring radjas. While the radja's strength of character, courage, public ascendancy in wealth, and other qualities guaranteed his own authority, it was never certain that his hasangapon would be inherited by his sons. The village inhabitants, seeking powerful central leadership, would — in most Batak tribes — reserve for themselves the choice of successor to a deceased chief. "Thus the sahala haradjaon did not automatically pass on from a man to one of his descendants or to a near kinsman."[38]

An alternative avenue to haradjaon was to establish a new *huta* (village) by pioneering uninhabited territory. "Founding a hoeta is an accepted method of gaining prestige, its objective is not so much material wealth but rather social standing."[39] With the assistance of his own clan and immediate relatives the founder constituted an example of the entrepreneur in traditional Batak society. Thus, although there was a strong conservative element in Batak religion there were also institutions of incisive socio-economic change such as that of the huta-founder in an entrepreneurial role.

Among the radjas the most powerful was Si Singamangaradja, recognized by most of Toba Batak society as their priest-king. The basis of his authority did not rest on force of arms or public council but on religious belief. This epic hero was commonly glorified in prayer and ceremony during festive occasions and lived on the shore of Lake Toba at Bakkara. All sorts of extraordinary occurrences were associated with his special power. His mother was said to have carried the first Singamangaradja seven years in the womb. To look upon his sword or hairy tongue would bring instant death. He could remain seven months without food, attended only by ancestral spirits, and could influence the weather and harvest. It was a common expression that "Si Singamangaradja is a visible god whose spirit we can know."[40] While the

---

38 *Ibid.*, pp. 288-89.

39 Justus M. Van der Kroef, "Entrepreneur and Middle Class in Indonesia," *Economic Development and Cultural Change*, II (January, 1954), 300.

40 Adniel Lumbantobing, *Sedjarah Si Singamangaradja I-XII* (Medan, Indonesia: Firman M. Sihombing, 1957), p. 10.

Singamangaradja did not follow Islam or Christianity, he claimed to follow the religion that was over all religions. The Singamangaradja dynasty lasted twelve generations, ending when the last heir died fighting the Dutch in 1907.

Si Singamangaradja seldom spoke but gave his orders in writing to be carried out by his personal representatives, organized into a *parbaringin* system throughout much of Batakland. He was known as an arbitrator between the autonomous villages in their disputes, seeking peaceful settlements and avoiding war. He was honored by the people for his ability to avert conflicts among them, and no Batak would mention his name without some fear for his terrible power. His standing throughout Batakland was compared to that of the pope in Europe in the Middle Ages. His financial resources were derived from voluntary donations by the various radjas and individual Bataks in return for special favors he would grant during periodic visits.

In each case of legitimized leadership among the Bataks, status was dependent on access to power and was associated with the religious system. "All who exhibit a particular power are always honored and respected by people as those deserving of respect, *na sangap*. Honor and respect, hasangapon, are the desirable results of possessing sahala."[41] But at the same time status was itself the source and justification of that power. Too often this meant that the mighty, with strong sahala and tondi, could do as they pleased while the moral commandments preached with such emphasis were binding primarily on the defenseless multitude.[42]

4. SOCIAL ORGANIZATION

For their protection against each other and to preserve the equilibrium of the microcosm the Bataks established a means of harmonizing the supernatural powers around them for their own welfare. This harmony was embodied in the notion of *adat*, which, while commonly translated "customary law," is actually a much more complex notion with consid-

---

41 Vergouwen, *op. cit.*, p. 83.
42 Warneck, *op. cit.*, p. 152.

erable religious meaning. The observance of adat was designed to avert disaster, restore harmony, promote fertility,
preserve health, and assure the welfare of the group. Mis-
haps, disasters, and strange phenomena of nature that threatened the welfare of the group were associated with violation
of the adat. Some attribute the adat's legal sophistication
to the frequency of quarrels among Bataks. When Si Radja
Batak, the first Batak, saw bitter quarrels among his sons,
he supposedly invented an intricate system of interpersonal
duties, privileges, taboos, expiations, and propitiations that
made up the Batak way of life and constituted his adat.[43]
Quarreling was not eliminated but directed through prescribed, legitimized channels attempting to maintain interpersonal relationships in all situations, working toward ultimate harmony of interest within the immediate community.
There was no provision for repentance, except if the vio-
lator could solicit the sympathy of a lenient judgment from
his indulgent accuser. Wrong behavior could expose the
individual and the whole community to unknown perils.
Morality was not a question of disposition but of external
behavior, not of moral conduct but of the performance of
a rite.[44]

Adat was enforced also by supernatural sanctions, with
deviations from adat bringing infertility, disease, and crop
failure. Thus, while any misfortune was considered punishment for some secret violation of adat, "a man with money,
good health, and many children has obviously fulfilled all
of his adat obligations."[45] Adat extolled the intelligence of
ancestors who formulated the laws and whose spirits enforced
their immutable authority. Until recently the Bataks would
contend that their adat had never changed in any fundamental
aspect, relegating progress and development to the non-adat
spheres of society. But the influences of Christianity, nationalism, and internationalism have forced the adat to be

---

[43] Johannes Keuning, *The Toba Batak, Formerly and Now*, pp. 3-4.
[44] Kraemer, *op. cit.*, p. 53.
[45] Edward Bruner, "The Toba Batak Village," in William G. Skinner,
Local, Ethnic, and National Loyalties in Village Indonesia, p. 55.

modified in order to survive. "One finds old ideas surviving where one would not expect them, and where one would presume there would be a tenacious adherence to old customs and beliefs, resistance to new influences is weak."[46]

A Batak author, writing on proposed changes, divided the adat into four categories.[47] First, there was the adat that restricted progress through expensive and elaborate feasts and ceremonies. Second, there was the adat that, as in careful ceremonial harvesting procedures, slowed progress but also contributed to the quality of production. Third, there was the adat that regulated community activities. Fourth, there was the adat ritual and symbolic practice that had aesthetic as well as functional value in society.

If the adat was changed irrespective of changing society, this would mean modifying social goals and values while retaining the social organization and status positions in the community. If the adat was to remain unchanged in the midst of social change, the goals and values of the adat system would remain static amidst a changing social organization. If both social change and adat change were to take place they would either change in the same direction to accommodate one another, or in different directions causing social conflict. Those who opposed modernization supported the adat against corrupting external influences, emphasizing ancestral traditions. Others tended to modify or reject the adat, regulating their social behavior according to alternative value systems.[48] Adat is the source of a Batak's identity. "We and our Adat are one. It is very difficult to explain yourself. So much does Adat mean in our lives."[49]

The efficacy of supernatural sanctions and the organization of social sanctions to enforce the adat have broken down in

46 Vergouwen, *op. cit.*, p. 3.

47 R. V. Simatoepang Siboerian, "Adat," in W. J. Ford and M. Ford van Lennerp, eds., *Indonesiers Spriken* (The Hague: Van Hoeve, 1947), pp. 104-105.

48 Harsja Wardjana Bachtiar, "Twelve Sumatran Villages: An Exercise in the Study of Political Institutions," unpublished M.A. thesis, Cornell University, June, 1959.

49 Sarumpaet-Hutabarat, *op. cit.*, p. 121.

Batak society. Before the revolution there was a "strong adat
with effective sanctions against the transgressor, an authoritarian colonial government, and another source of morality,
the church, administered by German missionaries."[50] Although
the adat continued to exert some control on society without
institutionalized external sanctions, its ability to enforce con-
formity was seriously diminished through social disorganiza-
tion following the Second World War and the Indonesian
Revolution. Prior to that time the authority of church, government and adat had reinforced one another's status in
society. One Batak radja discussing the appeal of Christianity
with Nommensen commented, "We are bad Bataks, for we
break our own laws. You have for the first time told us of
a way by which we can find strength to obey our Adat. If
Jesus can give us the power to be good Bataks, we want
Him as our Master."[51] The churches have been so willing
to accommodate aspects of the adat into their structure that
one of the Batak pendeta recently published an article entitled, "Have Bataks been Christianized, or Christianity Ba-
takized?"[52] He points out the careful preservation of pre-
Christian propitiations toward the ancestors, continued popu-
larity of the datu, and a tendency of Christians to overlook
and accommodate pre-Christian practices. He asks why, for
example, a prohibitively expensive adat feast is necessary
for a church wedding, and why, while accusations of unfaithfulness to adat inspire violent reaction, accusations of
unfaithfulness to Christianity are shrugged off.

The Batak churches have become increasingly concerned
about the role of the Christian in his adat. At a Seminar on
Adat and Christianity, held in July, 1968, a number of papers
were presented seeking to identify those aspects of adat which
complement Christian belief. Many of the ceremonies have
been retained in a modified form where prayers by the pendeta

---

50 Bruner, op. cit., p. 63.

51 Merle Davis, New Buildings on Old Foundations (New York: International Missionary Council, 1947), p. 43.

52 Pd. Poster Mula Pagoli Sibarani, "Batak Jang Dikristenkan Atau
Kristen Jang Dibatakkan?," Suara GKPI, March 1, 1966, pp. 13-15.

replace offerings by the datu, hymns replace the gondang gongs and collection of money replaces animal sacrifices. The ceremonies have generally been simplified, shortened, and made less expensive. The "humanitarian" reverence for ancestors has not been discouraged nor have those adat prescriptions which encourage a community spirit of mutual assistance. The monuments and "tugu" have been accepted as commemorative remembrances and the traditional gondang music, strictly prohibited by the church earlier, has been accepted for reasons of simple pleasure and honor.[53] When the churches have published prohibition of specific adat ceremonies they have included sufficient "exceptions" to the prohibition to leave the issue of Christianity and adat still deeper in ambiguity for the conscientious Christian.[54]

Even today the majority of Bataks seek to preserve the essentials of adat and participate fully in its regulations. Repeated transgressions may result in sharp criticism, social isolation, and possible expulsion from the genealogies of the Batak sib-group. In the process of modernization the urban Batak has become more Western in acceptance of technological improvements, material culture, and educational opportunities, and more Batak in retaining an up-dated version of the old adat value system. Anthropologist Edward Bruner cites five possible explanations for this phenomenon in the city.[55] First, many Toba Bataks have migrated to the city keeping their village system fairly intact within their group. Second, they are drawn together through feelings of in-group solidarity as an ethnic and Christian minority. Third, they have maintained close ties with their rural relatives. Fourth, they lack other alternative models of change and find that adat serves as a basis for moral order in society. Fifth, by

---

[53] "Mangongkal Holi Didalam Transisi Untuk Mendjadi Suatu Manifestasi Penghormatan Orang Tua Jang Bersifat Kememoratif," pp. 1-21 in Penindangion Hakristenon Di Adat, from the Adat Seminar, 27 July, 1 August, 1968 at Nommensen University, Pematang Siantar.

[54] "Synode Geredja Penta Kosta Indonesia Meeting in Pematang Siantar," Mimbar Umum, Medan, Tuesday, April 24, 1969.

[55] Edward Bruner, "Urbanization and Ethnic Identity in North Sumatra," in American Anthropologist, LXIII (1961), 519.

maintaining his adat the urban Batak maintains his sense of personal and cultural identity.

In the kinship structure there is first the nuclear family, then a minor lineage descending from one great-grandfather or great-great-grandfather, and finally a major lineage whose unity is based on common patrilineal descent from some ancestor who lived some six to ten generations ago. Beyond this is the *marga* (sib-group) of patrilineal descent going back to some ancestor who lived still further back, from whom the Batak draws his surname. Finally there are the two moieties Sumba and Lontung, the two sons of Si Radja Batak, ancestor of all Batak people. In traditional Batak society the localized lineage is based upon patrilocal residence and patrilineal descent and inheritance. Within that structure the affinal kinship relationships are carefully regulated by adat and provide a basis for social activity and a hierarchy for village leadership.

The nuclear family was largely absorbed into the localized lineage kinship system of the traditional village. The role of the woman in the nuclear family was highly ambiguous. "On the one hand she is treated as a commodity for sale, on the other she not infrequently stands forth adorned and jeweled."[56] The children were treated very permissively. "The child does not obey the parents, on the contrary, the parents will do anything the child may desire or demand."[57] It was felt that the child's tondi would be easily offended and likely to abandon the child if its demands were not met, resulting in illness or even death. Sibling relationships were also strictly regulated by adat avoidances where even the exchange of a few words in private between a man and woman would arouse the suspicion of the community. "Incest between family members is a thing to be avoided at all costs, as it would arouse the wrath of the gods and lead to disaster. The taboos therefore are strictest between brothers and sisters."[58] Overt sibling rivalry between brothers was a frequent

---

[56] Loeb, *op. cit.*, p. 71.

[57] Andar Lumbantobing, "Christian Education in the Batak Church," *Lutheran World*, II (Autumn, 1955), 291-96.

[58] Loeb, *op. cit.*, p. 51.

if not typical aspect of family life.[59] It was not the nuclear family but the clan that traditionally exerted a molding influence on children.

Every Batak is made aware of his own genealogical lineage by his family, community authorities on the adat, or through one of the numerous books that have been published tracing the lineage of Batak ancestors from twenty generations or more.[60] The patrimoieties, made up of all Bataks with the same marga surname, are divided into localized lineage groups. Since the localized lineages are rigidly exogamous, families are also integrated through affinal ties, thus providing a horizontal integration of society. The Bataks have a preferred ideal of matrilineal cross-cousin marriage that, although practiced less frequently today, maintains the lineage pattern in Batak society. "Thus in the villages the social system is based upon scattered localized lineages integrated vertically through descent lines and horizontally through affinal ties, providing a kinship grid covering the entire society."[61]

While the sense of group identity and social solidarity among village Bataks is very high, each jealously guards his particular status at adat ceremonies. The relevant hierarchy is clearly defined by the allocation of each specific part of the animal being eaten to the particular Batak in that status role.[62] Traditionally the circle of agnates was defined as *sisada sipanganon* (eating together as one), *sisada sinamot* (one in prosperity), *sisada hasangapon* (one in prestige), and *sisada hailaon* (one in humiliation).[63] The equalization of status was an important factor in maintaining unity throughout Batak society, although with increasing access to social,

---

59 Bruner, "The Toba Batak Village," *op. cit.,* p. 62.

60 I. J. Simandjuntak, *Pustaha Parturturan Batak* (Medan: Penerbit Tarubar, 1965); also Siahaan Mangaradja Asal, *Tarombo* (Medan: P. T. Siagian, 1962). (Numerous other books are also available in Sumatra.)

61 Edward M. Bruner, "Kinship Organization Among the Batak of Sumatra," *Transactions of the New York Academy of Sciences,* Series II, Vol. XXII, No. 1 (November, 1959), p. 120.

62 Vergouwen, *op. cit.,* pp. 88-89. Also note H. Th. Fischer, "Toba Batak Kinship Terms," *Oceania,* XXXVI, 4 (June, 1966), 253-63.

63 Vergouwen, *op. cit.,* p. 149.

political, and economic status outside the kinship system it has diminished in importance.

Those in the highest kinship status role, the *hula-hula*, were treated with great respect as representations of divine authority in society according to adat. In more recent years, however, the hula-hula were honored if very rich, but despised if poor. The Batak is apt to neglect a group that has diminished in numerical strength, wealth, power, and influence even though it is important from a genealogical standpoint, and to attach himself to another group that has become of more consequence in society. Nepotism has become a modern consequence of kinship ties in the city, where the marga serves as the social security, unemployment compensation, and insurance policy for the Bataks.[64]

Outside the kinship system there were three levels of political organization in traditional Batak society.[65] The *huta* (village) was led by a radja who had founded the village or a descendant of that founder. The *hordja* was a council of several villages with representatives chosen by participating village radjas. In the Karo Batak area, where the hordja council worked most effectively, the leaders were called Sibajak (exalted), while in the Simalungun area they carried the title of Tuhan (god) or Pertuhanan (godly). The *bius* was a collection of several hordja with every radja hordja being a bius representative. No permanent leader was selected for the bius, except for the duration of each meeting. Each of the two highest levels of organization, the bius and hordja, were called into action only when the general welfare of the community was in danger, as during epidemics or drought. The lines of direct authority followed genealogical rather than geographical lines with little infringement on the freedom and rights of virtually autonomous villages. While the hordja was organized among agnates, the bius was organized along geographical lines among the affines of a region.

---

[64] Clark E. Cunningham, *The Postwar Migration of the Toba-Bataks to East Sumatra*, p. 20.

[65] Adniel Lumbantobing, *op. cit.*, pp. 9ff.

5. Religious Organizations

Followers of traditional Batak religion can be divided among the Parmalims, the followers of Siradjabatak, and isolated individuals throughout Batakland not affiliated with any traditional religious organization. The Parmalims were organized in the late 1870s to preserve traditional beliefs against the corrupting influences of Christianity, Islam, and colonialism. The Parmalim sect, founded by the Singamangaradja, attracted followers from the Toba and Simalungun groups. The name was adapted from the Batak word *malim* (to be independent).[66] Somalaing, a high-ranking member of the parbaringan system, learned about Roman Catholicism from the Italian botanist Elio Modigliani, while acting as his guide in 1880, and incorporated many of these beliefs into the sect.

Another movement, called the Parhudamadam, was popular between 1907 and 1920 as an expression of opposition to foreign influence. The movement was inspired by the death of the last Singamangaradja, the imposition of heavy taxation by the Dutch, restructuring of land tenure patterns, and the spread of foreign influences throughout Batakland. It was particularly strong in the Karo and Simalungun regions. The movement was called "the new religion," surrounding the memory of Singamangaradja with a messianic mythology and the High God with a theme of apocalyptic destruction for nonbelievers. The movement spread through traveling teachers who proselytized villages much in the fashion of missionaries. The movement died out because it was unable to unite the diverse social, political, and religious interest groups among the Bataks, it was actively opposed by the Dutch military, and it was considered outmoded in the dynamic new Western value orientation of modernization.

On June 17, 1942, the Golongan Siradjabatak Indonesia movement was organized to call Bataks back to the religion of their ancestors. They proclaimed worship of the High

66 Justus M. Van der Kroef, "Messianic Movements in the Celebes, Sumatra and Borneo," in Sylvia L. Thrupp, *Millennial Dreams in Action*, pp. 99ff. Also note H. H. Bartlett, "Labors of the Datoe," *op. cit.*, pp. 15ff.

God, reverence of tribal ancestors, and preservation of adat. Drawing adherents from throughout Batakland for sacrificial festivals, a set of regulations was drawn up to preserve ancient traditions. The group drew most of its membership from Batak ancestor worshipers and those Christians under church discipline, but never succeeded in drawing a large following.[67] The followers of Siradjabatak incorporated many Christian beliefs into traditional religion and emphasized nationalism in its doctrines.

Philip Tobing expressed the hope that many Batak followers of traditional religion unaffiliated with organized ancestor worship groups might join the church, although he expressed disappointment that the Catholic Church was more active in their midst than the Protestants. Tobing predicted that by the 1970s, districts populated by unaffiliated individuals would become Roman Catholic, drawing many Protestants from these areas into Catholicism as well.[68]

The possibility of Batak unity was extinguished when the Toba, Simalungun, and Karo Bataks accepted Christianity while the Angkola and Mandailing groups turned to Islam. The antagonism became so strong that around 1920 the Mandailing Bataks initiated a campaign for separate recognition, that they might no longer be regarded as Bataks.[69] Islam was particularly active along the coastal borders of Batakland when Christian missionaries first penetrated the area. The Padri War of the 1820s brought Muslim armies of Imam Bondjol, or Tuanku Rao, from the southern Minangkabau stronghold of Islam as far north as Lake Toba, causing many Bataks to accept Islam along the way. There was a constant fear among Christian missionaries that they would arrive too late and that Islam, which was considered

---

[67] Andar Lumbantobing, "The Confession of the Batak Church," in Vilmos Vajta and Hans Weissgerber, *The Church and the Confessions,* p. 121.

[68] Philip L. Tobing, Letter of December 16, 1953, to Dr. Schiotz, Agenda, March 31, 1954, CYCOM, National Lutheran Council, Exhibit D, Indonesia, pp. 9-11.

[69] Keuning, *op. cit.,* pp. 3f.

a much more formidable opponent than ancestor worship, would block the advance of Christianity.

The Bataks were attracted to Islam for several reasons. Since coastal trade was for the most part in the hands of Muslims, it was an economic advantage to accept Islam. Islam offered the promise of education and entrance into modern society associated with the coastal cities. Missionaries commented on the underlying assumption that Islam was the religion of the future. "How often on the East Coast of Sumatra, when I asked the heathen if they were Mohammedans, did they answer: 'Not yet!' They were quite convinced they would be some day."[70] In any case, the Bataks recognized that their traditional religion was inadequate to cope with modern civilization. One Batak chief sent word to a Christian missionary in Central Sumatra, "Master, I must have a teacher. My old religion is no longer any use. It has outgrown itself and for a long time now I have ceased to believe in it. I must have a new one."[71]

The Dutch government inadvertently supported the advance of Islam. The progress of missions was severely restricted by the government, who feared "that the spread of Christianity might arouse the fanaticism of the Mohammedan and, thereby, make difficulties for the Government."[72] Later these restrictions were modified and the government sought help from the missionaries as allies. Many of the government institutions and staff were associated with Islam. The official language of office and school was Malay, often written in Arabic characters, and the civil servants as well as teachers were coastal Malays, all devout Muslims. While the Dutch were bringing new influences into Batakland, "the agents of civilization also for the most part wear the white turban, the badge of the worldly-wise Mecca pilgrim."[73] The association between civilization and Islam was so strong that

70 Simon, *op. cit.*, p. 223.

71 *Ibid.*, p. 286.

72 E. S. De Klerck, *History of the Netherlands East Indies* (Rotterdam: W. L. & J. Brusse, 1938), II, 390.

73 Simon, *op. cit.*, p. 34.

even Christian missionaries were obliged to assure Bataks they were not Muslims in disguise![74] However, the invasion of Muslim armies and centuries of social contact were unable to accomplish the Islamization of southern Batakland, which occurred spontaneously under the protection of the colonial government. By the middle of the nineteenth century an estimated one-fifth of the southern districts had been Islamized.[75]

In recent years Islam has changed its tactics. Formerly the Batak considered it a special favor if allowed to enter Islam and special doctrines protected his privilege to become Muslim "as long as he is ready to comply with the terms of admission."[76] In recent years the Jajasan Zending Islam (Islamic Missionary Institute) has been actively seeking the conversion of Bataks to Islam, even allowing reluctant converts to continue eating pork, an important delicacy in Batak adat feasts.[77]

It is ironic that the Muslim armies of Imam Bondjol invaded Batakland just as missionaries began to concentrate on the Bataks. While the invading armies did not convert more than the southernmost tribes they accelerated the breakdown of traditional Batak society. The missionaries were not hesitant to plant the seeds of Christianity in the newly ploughed fields of Batakland.

---

[74] *Ibid.,* p. 26.
[75] *Ibid.,* pp. 9-10.
[76] *Ibid.,* p. 13.
[77] Werner Grothaus, "Ein Volk im Aufbruch auf den guten Weg," in *Welt,* March, 1967, p. 5.

II

THE BATAK MISSION FIELD

1. MISSIONARY PENETRATION

THE MISSIONARY PENETRATION OF NORTH SUMATRA WAS A PHE-
nomenon of the nineteenth century. The Dutch East Indies
Company had established a congregation in 1679 at Padang
on the west coast but made no move to evangelize the indigenous population. With the arrival of the English in Java
and Sumatra in 1811 this policy was changed and missionary
work was tolerated if not encouraged.

Sir Thomas Stamford Raffles, the local British representative, strongly encouraged Christian missionary work among
the Bataks. Some sources claim Raffles was trying to divide
the strong Muslim Atjehnese to the North of Batakland from
the strong Muslim Minangkabau to the South.[1] This policy,
reputedly designed by Raffles and Lord Moira, who was British Governor General at Calcutta, was presumably part of the
divide-and-conquer pattern colonial powers were frequently
accused of following in Indonesia.

About this time the Baptist Mission Society of England sent
three missionaries to Sumatra. Richard Burton, a philologist

---

[1] Mangaradja Onggang Parlindungan, *Tuanku Rao* (Djakarta: Penerbit
Tandjung Pengharapan, 1964), p. 626.

and ethnologist, was assigned to translate the Bible into Batak; Nathaniel Ward, a hygienist, was assigned to evaluate the cholera plague that had reached epidemic proportions in Silindung and Toba; and Evans was assigned to establish schools around Tapian Na Uli. Arriving in 1820, Burton worked in Sibolga, Ward in Bengkulu, and Evans in Padang. Burton quickly learned the Batak language and translated almost half of the King James Bible into Batak script. By 1824 they were ready to explore Batakland.

Leaving Sibolga they traveled inland along the "Tappanooly" (Tapanuli) River, staying at Batak villages along the way. They were shown every courtesy as honored guests. When they arrived at the Silindung valley on May 4, 1824, with a group of radjas from a trading expedition, they were heartily welcomed. They accepted the hospitality of a radja from the valley and stayed until May 11, when they returned to Sibolga. The Bataks were more curious than hostile. The strangers were constantly accompanied by huge crowds and were able to preach to several thousand Bataks on at least one occasion. Because the cholera epidemic was still rampant in Toba and because they were so well received in Silindung, they canceled their original plan to visit Lake Toba. Burton and Ward reported how the Bataks considered themselves the original settlers in the region, coming from a country far to the east beyond the sea. The Sultan of Minangkabau was acknowledged as the ultimate sovereign over the local radjas. In his conjecture on the discussion between Burton and Ward with the Silindung radjas, a HKBP *pendeta* (pastor) recently suggested the Bataks' reaction might have been: "We do not feel able to leave our adat traditions, which have become part of our flesh. Not one part of this tradition can be changed. But if you will lead us to riches and glory we are ready to receive you and listen to you."[2] The result was

---

[2] Richard Burton and Nathaniel Ward, "Report of a Journey into Batak Country in the Year 1824," *Transactions of the Royal Asiatic Society,* I (1827), 485-513. Also note Ds. A. Silitonga, "Huria Kristen Batak Protestant Selajang Padang," *Oikumene, Geredja dan Masjarakat di Indonesia* (Djakarta: Badan Penerbit Kristen, 1965), p. 64.

that offers to evangelize and otherwise assist the Bataks were courteously rejected.

When Burton and Ward returned from Silindung they settled in Tapian Na Uli and helped Evans establish a school and orphanage. Missionary Burton later joined James Brookes as interpreter in negotiations with the Padri leader Tuanku Lelo, incurring the anger of the Dutch government and the British Baptist Mission. When the Tapian Na Uli territories were returned to the Dutch in 1824, Brookes, Burton, and other Englishmen were forced to leave by the Dutch government because of their sympathies with the Bondjol group and Tuanku Lelo.

Immediately after the visit from Burton and Ward came the Padri War, when Tengku Rau Bondjol from Central Sumatra invaded Batakland and secured a foothold for Islam in Tapanuli. The Batak villages as far as Lake Toba were ravaged in a way that was to provoke long-lasting antagonism against the Islamic regions to the South. The peace of all the Indies was thought to be threatened with a general Islamic uprising. The Netherlands Mission Society (NZG) sent the German missionary Karl August Gützlaff to evangelize in Sumatra, but due to the Padri uprising it was impossible for him to venture inland and he confined his work to the Chinese living in Batavia (Djakarta).

When the Dutch resumed control of Batakland they assigned an army chaplain, Colonel Elout, to evangelize Batakland. Along with another chaplain named Verhoeven, who had already begun work in the Mandailing area, Elout sought assistance from foreign missionary societies. Verhoeven began meeting with groups of Bataks at Pakantan and studied the Batak language. Verhoeven may have baptized the first two Bataks, Padri soldiers returned from Toba, in 1834, although the HKBP claims the first two Bataks to be baptized were Jacobus Tampubolon and Simon Siregar on March 31, 1861. Colonel Elout contacted the American Baptist Mission through his sister, then living in Boston, to send missionaries for work among the Bataks. He suggested that they would want to continue work abandoned by the British Baptists and might secure financial support from Boston shipping interests in return for trading concessions.[3]

About the same time, following up favorable reports by Dr. David Abeel who visited Java in 1831, the American Board of Commissioners for Foreign Missions (ABCFM) sent Henry Lyman and Samuel Munson to explore the interior of Sumatra. Munson, of New Sharon, Maine, was twenty-nine and Lyman, of Northampton, Massachusetts, was twenty-four years old. Munson was an alumnus of Bowdoin College, 1829, Lyman of Amherst, 1829. They had been classmates at Andover Theological Seminary, graduating in 1832. After a period of some months in Batavia (Djakarta) waiting for permission to enter Sumatra, where Munson studied Chinese and Lyman studied the Malay language, they parted from their wives and arrived in Sibolga on June 17, 1834. On Monday, June 23, they left Sibolga, following the steps of Burton and Ward to the Silindung valley.

Several factors are credited for American involvement in Sumatra at this time.[4] First, much attention had been drawn to the area through the capture of the American ship *Friendship* and the landing of United States marines at Kuala Batu in 1832. Second, the memoirs of Sir Stamford Raffles had just been published and this tended to encourage missionary efforts in Sumatra. Third, the ABCFM had just been highly successful in Bangkok and was taking a lively interest in Southeast Asia.

After Lyman and Munson left Sibolga there is some controversy about what exactly happened. The various accounts seem to indicate the following:

Leaving there on June 23 and travelling northward toward Lake Toba, they were to stay the night of June 28 with Radja

---

[3] Parlindungan, *op. cit.*, pp. 628ff. *Ibid.*, p. 626, claims that the Padri armies invaded Batakland from 1818 to 1820 and not from 1825 to 1829 as commonly reported. This would explain the Silindung Bataks' acknowledging Minangkabau sovereignty but would not fit with the general harmony Burton and Ward described among Silindung Bataks or with Burton and Ward's failure to mention such a devastating invasion in their accounts.

[4] James W. Gould, *Americans in Sumatra*, pp. 112-14.

Berampak at the Silindung village of Sukka, about 17 miles
northeast of Sibolga. En route that day they refused the advice of five armed Bataks who warned them to turn back.
Coming upon a log fort suddenly, the interpreter whom the
Dutch had supplied went forward and had a conversation
with occupants of the fort. No one has ever learned the subject of the talk. However, Munson and Lyman were immediately surrounded by two hundred armed men and killed.[5]

Since that time, in keeping with the reputation of the
Bataks, it has largely been assumed that Lyman and Munson
were eaten by the Bataks. There is no clear evidence that
this was in fact the case, and no eyewitness mentions actually
seeing the eating take place.[6] Dr. James Gould has carefully
researched alternate explanations of what might have happened. First, they may have been mistaken for being Dutch.
The reasons given by the Bataks for the act indicate that
the missionaries were suspected of being spies or enemies
seeking to destroy. At this time such an accusation would
imply their connection with the Dutch, who were extending
their influence into the Batak district. The Radja of Rau
had informed Lyman and Munson that they would be welcomed as long as they were not Dutch. Any such suspicions
would have been magnified by prevailing intervillage wars
following the Padri invasion and could have provoked the
violent act. While both foreigners were killed, all but one
of the accompanying natives escaped unharmed. Second,
there were reports at the time that Lyman and Munson were
killed by their own servants. If so, it would be difficult to
establish a motive, since theft of the inexpensive baggage
would not be sufficient cause and would probably have been
discovered later in any case. Third, some were suspicious that
the Dutch themselves may have been involved in the murder.
While the Dutch representative at Sibolga, Mr. F. Bonnet,
claims to have repeatedly warned the missionaries, letters
from Lyman and Munson indicate only his encouragement.
Bonnet had even threatened beforehand to punish anyone

---

[5] *Ibid.*, p. 113.
[6] *Ibid.*

spreading rumors the missionaries might be murdered. Ward had also reported earlier on how the Dutch had secretly opposed the efforts of missionaries despite outwardly friendly appearances. There was also much anti-American sentiment among the Dutch in the Indies at that time. Finally, there is evidence of a general tendency during the Dutch rule to discourage missionary penetration into the Indies. On the basis of the foregoing carefully collected evidence, Gould is dubious about the traditional explanation of the event as simply an incidence of Batak cannibalism.[7]

Mangaradja Parlindungan suggests still another alternative explanation. Lyman and Munson brought Kentucky long rifles with them to hunt deer for their meat supply. Near the village of Lobupining, Lyman accidentally shot and killed an old woman who was the aunt of Radja Panggulamai. Radja Panggulamai and a group of villagers immediately captured the missionaries, bound them to a tree, and, after some negotiations in which their guide Djamal Pasaribu spoke in their defense without success, killed them.

When the Bondjols invaded Batakland the Bataks remembered a sentence from Burton's sermon years before: "You must first decrease and become small and only then can you enter the Kingdom of God." The Bataks, having rebuffed Burton and Ward, concluded that he meant the Bondjol invasion to weaken the Bataks and had some part in this campaign. Consequently, the radjas in Silindung decided that in the future "the white eyes shall be forbidden to enter the area no matter from whence their origin." The murder of Lyman and Munson may have been related to this decision.

In the approximate area of the murder, on the border of the Silindung valley, the Bataks erected a memorial stone monument seventy-five years later on which is written the quotation from Tertullian: "The blood of martyrs is the seed of the Church."[8] At the centenary of the martyrdom on July 10, 1934, addresses were made by the Dutch Resident, representatives from the Rhenish Mission Society, and Bishop

[7] *Ibid.*, pp. 114-16.
[8] Th. Müller-Krüger, *Sedjarah Geredja di Indonesia*, p. 181.

Edwin F. Lee of the Methodist Episcopal Church, Singapore, who represented American Protestant missions in Sumatra. Although at that time the American Board suggested the inscription on the monument be changed to John 15:13 and others suggested John 16:1-3, the original inscription, mutilated by some unknown party, remains today.[9]

Immediately after the murder of Lyman and Munson, the American Board sent Jacob Ennis into the Batak area. Although well treated by the Bataks and meeting no difficulty, Ennis was discouraged by the Dutch from establishing a mission because of epidemic diseases spreading through the area. This was the last effort of the American Board to work in Sumatra.

By the time the Bondjol war was over, Islam had gained a permanent foothold in the southern Batak areas. Tengku Rau Bondjol succeeded in fighting off the Dutch around his Minangkabau stronghold and invaded Batakland deep into the Angkola, Silindung, and Toba regions, influencing many Bataks to join Islam. After the Dutch won, the government gradually began to establish sovereignty over surrounding Batak districts, sometimes by invitation and sometimes not. With the establishment of Dutch government rule over the area, there came a period of peace and order in southern Tapanuli around Mandailing and Angkola that was favorable to evangelization and further missionary work.

One of the first Westerners taking advantage of this opportunity to venture inland was the ethnologist F. Junghuhn, a German citizen, who led an expedition into the interior. Following his expedition he wrote, in 1847, the book *Beschrelbung der Battaländer,* one of the first careful studies of Batak culture and religion. As a result of reading Junghuhn's writings, Missionary Neubronner "Pondortuk" (Big Nose), as van der Tuuk was called, became interested in the Bataks. In 1849 he was sent by the Dutch Bible Society to stay in

9 Fred Field Goodsell, *They Lived Their Faith* (Boston: American Board of Commissioners for Foreign Missions, 1961), p. 217. Also note William E. Strong, *The Story of the American Board* (Chicago: Pilgrim Press, 1910), pp. 114-17.

Baros on the west coast of Sumatra. Van der Tuuk developed sufficient skill in the Batak language to write several books on Batak grammar, compile a dictionary, and translate several chapters of the Old Testament into Batak, which were later printed by the Dutch Bible Society. Van der Tuuk was a colorful figure, accepted by the Bataks almost as one of them. Enjoying special privileges, he may have been the first European to view Lake Toba. After he severed his connection with the Bible Society he worked as a linguist and ethnologist for the Dutch government, developing a Batak-Dutch dictionary. One apocryphal story about this eccentric individualist relates how he once received a cautious inquiry from Batavia about his progress and responded with a curt note that he was presently translating some violent Dutch obscenity into Batak!

Van der Tuuk offered radical advice to missionaries concerning the proper way to evangelize Batakland.

> There is no hope to be successful among the people of Angkola and Mandailing. The largest portion of them have already entered Islam, as have most of the Batak people under the governmental control of the Dutch. To spread Christianity, therefore, it will be necessary to take resolute action. All of the missionaries will have to be directed to other places. If we do not follow this plan, it is my opinion that the whole society will become Islamized before we realize it. Usually the Malayan language enters alongside governmental control, bringing many people from Malaya with the intention of converting these people to Islam.[10]

A congregation of Christian farmers in Ermelo, Holland, witnessed to their faith by sending F. van Asselt as an ordained worker to Sumatra. Asselt, who arrived in Padang in December, 1856, did not follow the advice of van der Tuuk and directed his attention toward southern Tapanuli. The Governor of West Sumatra put him to work on a government coffee plantation at Angkola, with the opportunity to evangelize in his spare time. Eventually, van Asselt moved to

---

10 Müller-Krüger, *op. cit.*, pp. 181-82.

Sipirok, which became a stepping-stone for the evangelization of Batakland.

From 1857 to 1861 van Asselt was followed by missionaries Dammerboer, who settled at Hutarimbarau (Angkola), van Dalen at Pagarutan (Angkola), and Betz at Bungabondar (Sipirok). The support from Holland gradually dwindled and the Sipirok work became financially dependent on the Organization for Home and Foreign Missions, located in Java. By 1864 the Java Committee had begun to support evangelization work in Sipirok. The Java Committee was originally sponsored by an Amsterdam group called the "Institute for Evangelization in the Church" for work in Java and Madura. In contrast to the state-supported Indonesian Protestant Church the Java Committee encouraged regional dialects over the use of the Malayan language and evangelization through a network of schools with increasing dependence on local financial support. When the HKBP was established as a legally independent church in 1931, the five thousand members under the care of Java Committee congregations around Sipirok merged with the HKBP.[11]

The Rhenish Mission Society (RMG) had been working in the Borneo area for about twenty-five years by this time. After the Borneo "Pangeran Hidayat" rebellion in 1859, the Dutch government severely restricted missionary work in Borneo. While in Holland to discuss possibilities for further evangelization in Indonesia, Dr. Fabri, the director of the RMG, came across the writings of Neubronner van der Tuuk. He immediately visualized the opportunity to enter an area where the language and customs were so well known, where the Bataks seemed ready to accept missionaries, and where Islam was about to gain control. Most of the missionary staff from Borneo were reassigned to Sumatra, together with several new missionaries from Germany.

On October 7, 1861, van Asselt gathered the Dutch missionaries at the home of Bondanalotot Nasution at Prau Sorat, Sipirok, to welcome the arriving German missionaries and

11 *Ibid.*, p. 182.

plan the evangelization of Batakland.[12] While the meeting was opened by the Dutch missionary van Asselt it was closed by the German missionary Klammer. The effort for Christianization of Batakland had passed from Dutch to German missionaries. This date was later fixed as the birth-date of the Huria Kristen Batak Protestant Church. Dutch missionaries Dammerboer and van Dalen refused to work under German leadership, and these men sought work as teachers under the Dutch government.

A Mennonite community was established at Pakantan, Mandailing, in 1838, erecting a Byzantine-style church there. Several Mennonite missionaries from the Russian Ukraine arrived at Pakantan between 1869 and 1918. The last Mennonite missionary, Iwan Tissanov, from the Russian group, moved from Mandailing to Bandung, Java, in 1918. The remaining Mennonite community followed the Java Committee into the HKBP in 1931. In 1951, however, the two hundred remaining descendants of these Mennonites separated again to form a distinct community.

2. DR. LUDWIG INGWER NOMMENSEN

Ludwig I. Nommensen was born on the island of Nordstrand in the Schleswig-Holstein region between Denmark and Germany on February 6, 1834, the year Lyman and Munson were killed. Pledging himself during a period of severe illness to be a missionary, this became his single-minded purpose in life. Upon his ordination in October, 1861, after training under the RMG, he set out for Sumatra. The voyage was a difficult one, and it was with some relief that he arrived at Padang on May 14, 1862, after a voyage of 142 days. Nommensen landed on the west coast of Sumatra just one year before Nienhyus, the son of an Amsterdam tobacco broker, landed on the east coast to establish large-scale tobacco plantations.[13] Nommensen's plan was to proceed inland immediately for work among the Bataks.

---

[12] Silitonga, op. cit., p. 66.

[13] Karl J. Peltzer, "Western Impact on East Sumatra and North Tapanuli," Journal of South East Asian History, II, 2 (1961), 66-71.

The missionary Denninger and his wife, who were later to start missionary work on the island of Nias just off the west coast of Sumatra, were Nommensen's first contacts in Padang. Denninger was unable to secure permission from the Dutch government to work in the interior but could operate only along the coastal regions, a restriction that also applied to Nommensen and frustrated his plan to proceed inland. Furthermore, the Dutch and RMG missionaries already on the field had decided at their meeting in Sipirok that missionary activity should concentrate on southern Tapanuli, which was also contrary to Nommensen's intentions. Finally, Nommensen secured permission to work at Baros, the northernmost outpost of the Dutch government. Baros was considered a miserable place to live, and the only Europeans there were the police officer and controller. The rest of the population was a mixture of Chinese merchants, fanatical Malay Muslims, and several Batak traders.[14] Nommensen viewed this as a temporary position, while he established contacts and continued to study the Batak language. His medical skill through "homeopathy" enabled him to spend his time living among the Bataks, serving their physical as well as spiritual needs. Isolated from other missionaries Nommensen lived an extremely simple life of self-denial, but was adamantly unwilling to establish himself where other missionaries were already active when such a large area of non-Christian Sumatra lay before him. His plan was to live entirely off the local economy and eventually establish a Christian colony that could provide itself with all necessities.

Nommensen's first journey inland began on October 25, 1862, and was highly successful. He made many friends, was welcomed nearly everywhere he went, and was invited back to establish himself in several villages. With a plan to establish a colony at Rampe and another at Tapa, he wrote to the RMG in Barmen to send another missionary. But when the Resident

14 J. H. Hemmers, "Sketches from the Life of Nommensen, The Apostle to the Bataks," translated by R. L. Archer and serialized in *The Malaysia Message* from November, 1935, to October, 1939. This reference is from November, 1935, p. 13.

of Sibolga learned that Nommensen had traveled so far beyond the limits of Dutch territory his disapproval was very
evident and the permission for settlement was emphatically
denied.[15]

Nommensen then decided to move to Sipirok, where missionaries were now permitted to work, and penetrate inland from
that point. In Sipirok, however, his fellow missionaries assigned
him to establish a school at Prau Sorat, where the Muslims
had gained influence. Nommensen's second journey inland, in
November, 1863, was to the region of Silindung. The missionaries van Asselt and Heine had visited the region in 1862 and
vividly described the tremendous potential for missionary activity from that centralized location throughout the northern
regions. They had made contact with many friendly radjas,
among them Radja Pontas Lumbantobing, and had proceeded
as far as Sipoholon without encountering any difficulty. Furthermore, work at the Prau Sorat school was going badly due to
competition with both Muslim and government schools.

Nommensen, accompanied by Missionary Betz, started out
to the border of Dutch territory. The area was in turmoil at
this time with considerable intertribal warfare, although Nommensen was generally well received. Venturing as far as Sipoholon, he met his first real opposition from those who thought
him a representative of the Dutch or perhaps some evil spirit
because of his "goat eyes," goats being the only other blue-
eyed creatures many Bataks had ever seen. Learning of Nommensen's intention to live in Silindung, the radjas were
openly hostile, but finally they agreed to let him settle in
the valley. His friendly manner and medical skill helped him
to bridge this gap of misunderstanding and he made many
friends, among them Ompu Jarida and Radja Ompu Tonggul.

For much of his journey he was accompanied by Radja
Pontas Lumbantobing, who acted as his guide. Radja Pontas
Lumbantobing considered the Singamangaradja dynasty to
have legitimately ended with the death of Si Singamangaradja
X in 1819 and was generally opposed to the reigning Si
Singamangaradja XII. In recognizing the need for moderniza-

---

[15] *Ibid.*, January, 1936, p. 14.

tion and monotheism he became a chief ally of the early
missionaries. When Radja Pontas Lumbantobing was baptized by Nommensen on August 27, 1865, he was the first
person of authority in northern Batakland to accept Christianity.

Having achieved his objective, Nommensen returned to
Angkola to make preparations for the move. His colleagues,
however, informed him that before he would be allowed to
settle in Silindung, he would have to work with Missionary
Betz on evangelization and education at Prau Sorat. When
they finally allowed him to return to Silindung, conditions
had changed. The villages were fortified against attack, guards
were stationed along the way, and there were rumors of war.
Many threats were made against Nommensen, and he encountered stiff opposition. One of the radjas tested Nommensen with a riddle. "If a person scatters grains of rice on the
road do not the birds of the sky come and pick them up?"
To this Nommensen replied, "But if you continually keep
driving the birds away they will be unable to pick up the
scattered grains of rice."[16]

Nommensen's attempts to establish himself were constantly
frustrated. It seemed that previous visits from white foreigners were always followed by natural disasters such as epidemics, crop failure, or earthquakes. The cause of these disasters was thought to be that the white foreigners did not
observe the adat, so it became adat not to receive white
men as guests. Living in a rice barn, Nommensen tried to
build a house but could not secure either land or building
materials. He tried to establish a school, but no children
would attend. Finally he gained the confidence of Radja Aman
Dari, who, with three other radjas, made "an alliance of
sharing life and death equally with Dr. Nommensen."[17]
Nommensen finally secured some swampland and purchased
lumber from an abandoned building to erect his own house,

16 *Ibid.*, June, 1936, p. 13.
17 Philip L. Tobing, "Dr. Nommensen and the Rapid Christianization
and Development of North Tapanuli in Sumatra," *De Heerbaan,* September 10, 1964, p. 244.

but he continued to receive hostile threats from his neighbors. Then one day Nommensen called all the radjas in the area to assemble and showed them his stamped government permit to visit the region, threatening to record the names of all those who would oppose him. The Dutch were greatly feared by the Bataks and their authority commanded considerable respect, which consequently modified the opposition.[18]

There were elements in the Batak character that Nommensen found difficult to understand. One day he drank coffee with a Batak who impressed him favorably as a man of good character. But a few days later he met that same man "leading a blood-thirsty band by the side of a man who in one hand carried a freshly cut human head stuck on the end of a bamboo pole and in the other hand the dead man's arm from which several fingers were missing."[19]

On another occasion a great feast was called to honor the sombaon Si Atas Barita, at which Nommensen was himself to be the sacrifice. On September 23, 1864, in the midst of the feast and after the medium had worked the crowd up to a pitch of excitement calling for his blood, Nommensen walked into their midst and proclaimed to the assembly that it was Satan, not their ancestor Si Atas Barita, who was speaking to them through the medium. Then he confronted them with their own customary laws of hospitality and adat to support his claim. The combination of his courageous direct confrontation and familiarity with their own adat impressed the assembly and Nommensen was not harmed. The next day Nommensen's chief opponent was killed by enemies of a neighboring village and an unusually heavy rain fell on the area, which were both taken as signs that the "white-eyes" had won and God was on his side. Nommensen sent the message to Barmen that "Silindung lies open before us. The Bataks wish you to send more missionaries."[20]

Gradually Nommensen came to know the Bataks, comprehend their unique logic, and win their confidence, so that

18 Hemmers, *op. cit.*, July, 1936, p. 13.

19 *Ibid.*, November, 1936, p. 20.

20 *Ibid.*, December, 1936, p. 29.

even those who were unsuccessful in their attempts to kill him were converted to Christianity. Nommensen became increasingly involved in settling local disputes as the people began to accept his presence.[21] In addition, he was kept busy caring for the sick and establishing a school, reaching the parents through their children. At first he would preach on Old Testament Bible stories whenever the Bataks came together for market days and feast days, until it was made clear to him that these traditional assemblies should be left undisturbed and that they would prefer him to visit them at home.

Nommensen baptized his first converts, four men, four women, and five children, on August 27, 1865. These converts, and those who followed, were expelled from their villages and came to Nommensen for help. It became necessary to change the mission station into a small village, with drains and earthen walls in the prescribed manner of a Batak huta. Although Nommensen had once hoped to establish a Christian colony, he now had serious objections to this enforced isolation of Batak Christians from the common life of their people. Huta Dame (Village of Peace), as the village was called, contained a modest church, a school building, and several other houses. Having established a village, Nommensen, according to adat, became a radja himself and was held responsible for the behavior of his villagers. This was to cause considerable difficulty for Missionary Nommensen, who did not wish to be placed in that position of secular authority. Huta Dame soon encountered many problems. One problem was a smallpox epidemic, which broke out in March, 1866, just as Nommensen's fiancée and Missionary P. H. Johannsen arrived from Germany to assist Nommensen. Dozens of children in neighboring villages died, but fortunately none of the inhabitants of Huta Dame died, causing many families to bring their sick children to Huta Dame for treatment.

One day Nommensen received word that the Singamangaradja was gathering an army at Sipoholon to destroy Huta Dame and kill all the Christians on July 27 or 29, 1866. It

21 *Ibid.*, February, 1937, p. 21.

seems that all the evil spirits had moved to Toba where Si
Singamangaradja lived, since the Christians had made things
too difficult for them in Silindung. The Singamangaradja
had such power that even those radjas friendly to Nommensen were afraid to oppose him directly. The whole village
prepared for their inevitable destruction. However, in his
eagerness, the Singamangaradja neglected certain necessary
ritualistic ceremonies and the radjas were so incensed by
this negligence that they refused to obey orders.

Civil disorder in the Batak area was a constant source of
frustration. At one point the war fever increased to the point
that Nommensen requested the resident Dutch government
official at Sibolga to come and put an end to the hostilities.
The Resident refused to become involved in Batak affairs,
and "since that was an independent territory the Dutch Government could not come in to settle their disputes."[22] These
conditions of uncertainty may have contributed to the feeling
by members of the Mission Committee that Nommensen was
proceeding too fast in his program of evangelization.

Nommensen received repeated warnings from Barmen
against attempting too rapid progress, which the Mission
Society feared might lead to disaster in Sumatra as it had
previously in Borneo. It was a constant source of annoyance
to Nommensen that Barmen failed to recognize the urgency
of his immediate opportunities and would attempt to guide
his program from distant Europe. There were not only the
traditional forces to contend with, but also rapidly increasing
efforts by Islam to win influence in Batakland. It was difficult
to determine the motives of these rapidly accumulating converts, but the people were accepting Christianity in increasing numbers and it was difficult to refuse baptism to those
who had decided to break with their own traditions. Such
refusal might drive potential converts to Islam and create an
even greater difficulty. Nommensen felt that "God's time
for the Batak" had arrived.

The Dutch soon began to take an interest in Nommensen's
work, and in November, 1868, Governor Arriens of Padang

sent word that he would be visiting the Silindung valley and would stop at the mission station of Huta Dame.[23] This message had an instantaneous effect on the Bataks. Some feared a repetition of the Bondjol invasion. Others ran away in fear of being punished for crimes they had committed. Everyone, except Nommensen, was apprehensive concerning the forthcoming visit. The greatest effect the visit had, however, was a decree establishing a Christian as radja of one nearby village, and another declaring that all children under fourteen years of age, born of slave parents, should be recognized as free.

An important aspect of Nommensen's program was his emphasis on social concerns. He established a medical center at Huta Dame and planned to establish mission colonies in the valley that could engage in large-scale business enterprises, hoping to introduce modern agricultural techniques in the process. He frequently paid the ransom for slaves destined to be killed, loaned money at a low rate of interest, healed the sick, and was known for his willingness to withstand insult and even help those who insulted him. The spiritual and social were closely aligned in Nommensen's mind. "For when the spiritual message has been accepted, the people become more conscious of the social misery in which they have been living."[24]

Whenever possible, Nommensen sought to accommodate Batak adat into the new Christian way of life. He continued many of the marriage customs regulated by kinship structure, he tolerated such customs as filing of teeth (hoping they would die out by themselves), and substituted hymns and a brass band for traditional tribal music. Nommensen recognized the authority of adat law in the constantly recurring civil disputes and provided places of special authority in the Christian hierarchy for those persons of influence and radjas who joined the church. At the same time Nommensen encouraged the Dutch government to prohibit the Singamangaradja parbaringan organization and those ceremonies of traditional religion which focused Batak opposition to the church and

---

23 *Ibid.*, p. 19.
24 *Ibid.*

government. Among the innovations he introduced were a "walking school" where students spent a day or two with Johannsen at Pansurnapitu, Nommensen at Huta Dame, and Mohri at Sipoholon; a loan service to wipe out the injustice of usury; and in 1882 a training school where the more promising Batak teachers could study for ordination to the ministry. "Until this time no mission society in Sumatra had thought of training an ordained native ministry."[25]

In a letter to Barmen, Nommensen spoke of a vision he had for the future of this new Christian community.

> In spirit I see scattered everywhere Christian congregations, schools and churches, groups of Bataks old and young, making their way to these churches: on every side I hear the sound of church bells calling the believers to the house of God. I see everywhere cultivated fields and gardens, green pastures and forests, tidy villages and dwellings in which are found properly dressed descendants of this people. Still more, I see preachers and teachers, natives of Sumatra, standing on the platforms and behind the pulpits, pointing out the way of the Christian life to both young and old. You will say that I am a dreamer, but I say, No! I am not dreaming. My faith visions all this; it shall come to pass for all kingdoms shall be His and every tongue shall confess that Christ is Lord to the glory of God the Father. Therefore, I am encouraged, though the people may oppose me and make all sorts of plans to resist God's word they can just as easily keep the ocean back from its shores as to keep God's word from their hearts. A stream of blessing shall certainly flow over them. Already the day begins to appear. Soon the clear light will break forth and then shall the Sun of Righteousness in all His glory shine over the horizon of Batakland from the South even to the shores of the Toba Sea.[26]

The Bataks frequently found Singamangaradja's dream of driving the white man out of the country easier to believe than Nommensen's vision. First the missionaries and now the Dutch were beginning to establish themselves and undermine both secular and sacred traditional authority. In preparation

---

[25] *Ibid.*, January, 1938, p. 18.
[26] *Ibid.*, April, 1938, p. 12.

for his big assault Si Singamangaradja hired a number of soldiers from Atjeh to help him, circulating rumors that the Sultan of Turkey would attack from the south and soon all Sumatra would be freed from the white man. The old Singamangaradja had made a peace covenant with Nommensen and even requested that a European wife be provided for him. But his heir, Singamangaradja XII, had a more militant view toward foreigners, especially since the missionaries had begun to move into the Toba region.

The Dutch Resident, alarmed by rumors that all Christians and missionaries were about to be killed, sent a hundred soldiers from Singkel with extra guns and ammunition. On the day officially announced for the battle, some six hundred Batak warriors descended on Bahal-Batu, but they were driven back. When the Resident from Sibolga arrived with two hundred more troops, the Dutch decided to counterattack the Singamangaradja, burning villages on the way. After a series of encounters the Bataks were convinced that further resistance would be useless and requested that hostilities cease. Nommensen and his colleagues played an important role in mediating that peace. The arrival of two hundred more Dutch troops also had an effect. An assembly of radjas acknowledged the authority of the Dutch, who then withdrew, leaving a garrison of eighty men at Laguboti and a district officer at Tarutung. "From that time on the missionaries were relieved of responsibility as judges for the Bataks since thereafter all disagreements in Silindung were investigated and adjusted by constituted government authority."[27]

In 1883 the Singamangaradja tried for the last time to drive the Dutch and the missionaries out of Toba. He hired a number of Malay troops and secured a large following of Bataks to attack Balige on the shore of Lake Toba. A number of missionaries in stations near Lake Toba were evacuated; but after a brief engagement the Dutch garrison drove the Bataks off and followed up this action with an invasion of the Singamangaradja's stronghold at Bakara, eliminating any strong, organized opposition to Dutch rule.

---

[27] *Ibid.*, May, 1938, p. 13.

In 1881, returning from a furlough in Europe, Nommensen
was given the title of "Ephorus" (overseer) by the RMG,
which is still retained as the title of supreme authority in
the HKBP. In 1904 he was granted an honorary degree of
Doctor of Theology by the University of Bonn. His greatest
accomplishments, however, were less spectacular, using local
resources in Batak villages and churches. "He felt that a
teacher or pastor who was paid for by some outside source
could only dull the edge of an independent Church."[28] The
policy of using indigenous leadership perhaps more than any
other factor prompted the mass conversion of Bataks to Christianity. Many of the missionaries were apprehensive about
the rapid conversion of Bataks, but Nommensen felt that
"now it was their task not to fish with a hook but with a
net."[29] When Nommensen died, on May 23, 1918, the church
had grown to include about 180,000 baptized members, the
510 schools had an enrollment of 32,700 pupils, and the
church was led by 34 ordained Batak pendeta, 788 teachers,
and 2,200 elders.[30]

3. The Christianization of Tapanuli

Christianity arrived in a context of rapid social change and
social disorder throughout Batakland. The Dutch government
was able to influence if not control activities in southern
Tapanuli, where missionary work was already established; but
only the ports of Sibolga and Baros in northern Tapanuli
were directly under Dutch influence. With the growth of
Dutch influence, plantations were being established, breaking
down the regional isolation. Remembering van der Tuuk's
advice about the importance of preceding Dutch influence,
southern Tapanuli became a gateway for missionary activity
to the northern interior. Evangelization became a contest between Christianity and Islam for the Batak.

While pushing farther North the missionaries also continued to consolidate their position in the South. Working

---

28 Müller-Krüger, op. cit., p. 187.
29 Ibid., p. 189.
30 Lehman, Gottes Volk im vielen Ländern, p. 143.

from their first base at Sipirok, the influence of missionaries continued to the Bunga Bondar and Sipiongot area, in the jungle region of Padang Bolak. The Java Committee, led by Dutch missionaries, had congregations at Huta Imbaru and Pargarutan, but, except for using the Heidelberg Catechism, their work differed little from that of the RMG.

The Silindung valley became a new gateway for Christianity. Two years after the radjas from Balige had requested missionaries from Nommensen and after the safety of missionaries had been guaranteed by the radjas and enforced by the presence of a Dutch Controller at Tarutung, missionaries Pilgram and Kessel moved to Balige on the shore of Lake Toba to begin working. They were amazed at how much the Bataks there already knew of the Christian faith, indicating how rapidly this new message was spreading out before them. But missionaries were not always welcome. When Missionary Bonn arrived to work at Muara, on Lake Toba, the people insulted him and sought to provoke him. The situation finally became so dangerous that three other missionaries were sent to work with him. Other dissidents succeeded in burning the church at Sipoholon and the meeting hall at Tarutung as well as the missionary's house at Simorangkir. But new churches were erected and guarded by the Christian converts.

By 1881 the missionaries decided to call a "Conference of Christian People" at Pearadja near Tarutung to plan for the future and demonstrate their growing strength to the surrounding community. The meeting, attended by 3,500 Christians, was significant in welding this group of early converts into a church. Large numbers of Bataks were now joining the church, requiring more personnel for the Silindung and Toba region. The missionary conference in 1903 decided to send evangelists across Lake Toba and farther North, including the area of the Simalungun Bataks in East Sumatra where giant plantations were just opening up. Sending this suggestion to Barmen for confirmation, they received the one-word, cabled response *"Tole!"* (Onward!). Finally, the areas to the west of Lake Toba were opened up in Dairi and Pak-Pak, which the Dutch had pacified by 1917.

Christianity reached the borders of Batakland around the year 1920, but there were still more than a hundred thousand Bataks who were not Christianized. This was especially true in the remote regions of Dairi Samosir, Simalungun, and the Islamic areas of Angkola and Mandailing. Traditional religion had declined in influence by this time, and many Bataks were ready to receive a new religion, either Christianity or Islam.

Although the Dutch government exerted an important influence in the region, the officials generally maintained a carefully neutral position in religious matters. The Dutch entered the Batak area eleven years after missionary work had begun, but after their arrival the missionaries found the Dutch presence a real advantage. The disturbing influence of the Singamangaradja had been suppressed and government presence ended the incessant tribal wars.

Nommensen stubbornly asserted an independent policy for himself and the developing church against the control of the RMG in Barmen. Many German missionaries were hesitant to place authority in the hands of their recent converts. This was partly because of a patriarchal theory of the ministry; partly due to an attitude of racial superiority among some missionaries who sincerely, although mistakenly, believed these converts-incapable of spiritual progress; and partly because of the missionaries' pietistic view of the church as a gathering of visible saints, leading missionaries to expect a high order of spiritual discipline. "Simple trust in Christ was replaced by the missionaries' ideal of self-reliance. Faith in the re-creating power of the Gospel was replaced by educational requirements and the biblical concept of sanctification was replaced by considerations of the human qualifications of the native Christians."[31]

Evangelization proceeded from one Batak tribe to the next, spreading from Mandailing-Angkola, to Toba, to Simalungun, and finally to the Pak-Pak. While the influence of Islam and traditional religion was still strong in other areas, the Toba

---

[31] Peter Beyerhaus and H. Lefever, *The Responsible Church and the Foreign Mission*, p. 121.

and Silindung society was so thoroughly Christianized that to be a Batak was also to be a Christian.

As large numbers of Bataks joined the church, the same strong family feeling and corporate identity that, in the beginning, had made individual conversion so difficult now facilitated mass conversion of Bataks to Christianity. The phenomenon of regional conversion in Batakland has been described as a "mass-movement" to Christianity. The anthropologist Alan Tippett, lecturing at the School of World Mission and Institute of Church Growth, Fuller Theological Seminary, is critical of the term "mass-movement" as applied to rapid growth in Batak church membership. He considers these conversions as multi-individual decisions following discussion as the unanimous action of a group, in accordance with adat regulations. Tippett equates the term "mass-movement" with the unitary response of a startled herd of kangaroos bounding off without knowing why. Tippett prefers the terms "multi-individual" or "people-movement" to describe Batak church growth. The issue of proper terminology is still under debate.

Although the majority of converts openly confessed that they came simply because their companions came, the missionaries decided not to turn them away. Instead, they provided a period of probation and instruction so that the converts could learn about Christianity and give evidence of their sincerity. "In the Batak Mission those who are willing to break utterly with heathenism are admitted to the catechumenate, i.e., are permitted to share in public worship and in the somewhat long course of instruction for baptism."[32] To make up for the lack of missionary personnel during the First World War there was increased reliance on laymen and indigenous Christians in leadership roles. Church leadership was drawn from the heads of clans and villages, who had sometimes acted as priests in the worship of ancestors under traditional religion. "They were invested with responsibility

---

[32] Johannes Warneck, "The Growth of the Church in the Mission Field," *International Review of Missions,* I (1912), 23.

in matters of Church government and Church discipline, in the settling of quarrels among Christians, in the fixing of Church rates, and the erection of Church buildings."[33] Schools were established to train teachers and candidates for the ordained ministry. Although at first the curriculum was burdened with too much European learning, eventually the course was boiled down to four years of training for teachers and two additional years for preachers. The ideal of the mission was "the Christianizing of Sumatra by Christian Sumatrans."[34]

A widespread system of outstations was established to serve the remote areas, and institutions were established in the more populated regions including a girls' school managed by German deaconesses, 494 public schools, 200 vocational training schools, a technical school, and a Dutch middle school. These institutions and the mission program could not have been realized "without the generous support of the Dutch Colonial Government, which made a yearly grant to the schools of eighty thousand florens and thereby enabled the Mission, which was not well supplied with funds, to erect good schools, keep them in repair, and supplement the small salaries of the teachers."[35]

With the outbreak of the First World War all financial help from Germany was stopped and the mission was faced with the threat of extinction until the Netherlands Indies government agreed, on certain conditions, to provide financial help. In exchange, the mission was required to limit its program to the work in hand, since funds would be provided only for existing work. This meant that no new missionaries could come out and missionaries on the field could not go home.[36] Consequently, still more responsibility was placed in the hands of indigenous workers.

The policy of increased dependence on indigenous leader-

33 *Ibid.*, p. 25.
34 *Ibid.*, p. 26.
35 *Ibid.*, p. 27.
36 Hemmers, *op. cit.*, October, 1939, p. 17.

ship was less a deliberate, enlightened strategy of any single missionary or mission society and more an expedient adaptation to necessity. With the mass movement to Christianity the need for more personnel was great and the availability of foreign missionaries very limited. The missionaries had no choice but to trust new converts with the responsibilities of leadership. While Nommensen and later Warneck recognized the advantages of this policy it is doubtful they could have instituted such a strategy if political conditions had not made such a policy an expedient necessity.

The mass movement also gave rise to organizational problems. There was a deliberate attempt to avoid stereotypes of Western Christianity as dangerous to the life of a Batak church. The individual congregation was made a basic unit in the organization, with its council of elders and teachers who, under the supervision of a missionary, were responsible for congregational maintenance and local decisions. The council system was extended to two provincial synods, one body made up of elders and another of teachers and preachers. These two synods reported annually to an association of missionaries, who received their recommendations.

Adaptation of indigenous social customs also constituted a problem, with the mission taking the view that every native custom "which is not directly contrary to the Christian spirit should be allowed to continue in order that all unnecessary conflict with popular feeling may be avoided and the way to Christ, already difficult enough, may not be needlessly encumbered."[37] Although every attempt was made to avoid Europeanizing the Batak Christians, the church building, bell, clerical robe, and hymnody stand out as clear symbols of Western Christianity. The church was to grow out of local society and economic support. The goal of independence was to be realized through self-support, self-government, and complete self-maintenance. The mission looked forward to a day when the Batak church could dispense with missionaries. Warneck, a chief architect of this policy, kept "in view that

---

37 Warneck, *op. cit.*, pp. 29-30.

our object is not to drill, but to educate, not to produce imitators but intelligent personalities with strong wills, capable of acting and judging for themselves."[38]

---

[38] *Ibid.*, p. 30.

III

THE BATAK FOLK CHURCH

1. BATAK MISSIONARIES

WITH RAPID GROWTH OF CHRISTIAN INFLUENCE AMONG TOBA
Bataks came the hope that all Bataks would one day unite
in a single church. The mass movement to Christianity rapidly
spread from the Silindung valley to the area surrounding Lake
Toba and beyond to the Simalungun Bataks. Christians from
Angkola, Mandailing, Toba, Simalungun, and Pak-Pak tribes
were gathered together in a single Batak church that adopted
the name Huria Kristen Batak Protestant in 1930. Some
missionaries and many Batak Christians hoped that this organization would become the church for all those Batak tribes
whose culture and language shared the same ethnic heritage.

The desire of each individual tribe to be independent frustrated any ideal of a Batak folk church, leading to divisions,
disagreements, and the entrance of other missionary organizations. In the districts of the HKBP to the South (Angkola)
and to the Northeast (Simalungun) the laity were especially
dissatisfied as members of a fellowship dominated by 75 percent Toba Bataks. Later the Simalungun Bataks were given
separate status within the HKBP. In response to the various
factions five districts were established and expanded to thir-

teen after 1940. This approach did not entirely eliminate the centrifugal force of tribal factionalism, however.

The ideal of a Batak church was never realized, and instead many different Batak churches have developed. In some cases these churches have developed along tribal lines, with the Toba, Simalungun, and Karo Bataks remaining organizationally separate. In the formation of most other churches, however, membership crosses tribal lines, and they draw members from many Batak tribes. Allocation of comity by the Dutch government according to tribal lines enhanced tribal differences. At the same time, the fragmentation of churches reflects pre-Christian ethnic divisions and intertribal antagonism, which made it "sometimes difficult for one part to feel its responsibility for other parts."[1] Just as the Toba Bataks, through the Singamangaradja and parbaringan system, served as the religio-cultural center of Batak society, so the Toba-led HKBP focused the identity of Batak Christians. The idea of a single institution encompassing all Batak people was, however, foreign to traditional Batak society and modern Christian community alike. The Bataks have been more attracted to local autonomy and decentralized organization, resulting in a plurality of churches.

While the HKBP was never able to unify all Batak churches it served to nurture Christianity in Batakland and became a source of trained personnel and status for other emerging churches. The enthusiasm and courageous dedication of HKBP members became an important factor in the spread of Christianity throughout Batakland. The first elders appointed by Nommensen were assigned exclusively to missionary work and spread the gospel from village to village. As early as 1899 Pendeta Henok Lumbantobing founded the Kongsi Batak or Pardonganon Mission Batak (Batak Mission Association) to evangelize the island of Samosir and around Lake Toba.[2] The Batak church delegated evangelization in new regions to this organization which was outside the church structure. At first

---

[1] E. Verwiebe, "The Batak Church in Sumatra," in *The Growing Church*, Tambaram Madras Series (London: Oxford, 1939), II, 134-35.

[2] *Almanak Ni Huria Kristen Batak Protestant HKBP*, 1965, p. 332.

the organization failed to prosper, but after 1921 when the name was changed to Batak Zending (Batak Mission) and the organization was incorporated into the church structure it proved extremely successful.[3] The organization was designed to work exclusively among Bataks with particular attention to the many Bataks migrating throughout the Indies. In 1903 a Batak pendeta and three teachers began work on the island of Enggano, resulting in several congregations now members of the HKBP. Working with the RMG on the Mentawei Islands off the west coast of Sumatra, the missionary organization founded a church that had grown to 1,100 members by 1940. After the Second World War two Mentawei teachers, educated at the HKBP seminary at Sipoholon, established their own independent church, which has retained a relationship with the HKBP and the RMG and is now called Paamiam Kristen Protestant Mentawei.[4]

More recently the missionary organization began work among the Sakai tribes of Central Sumatra. These people were the original inhabitants of Sumatra before the Malayan migrations with a history dating back to at least 1,000 B.C. The Batak pendeta Simandjuntak with several coworkers is actively engaged in this promising work, which now includes a school and several congregations.

Missionary work was not limited to isolated islands or rural areas. In 1907 a graduate from the seminary at Pansurnapitu with the name of Hasibuan began work in Batavia (Djakarta), and by 1909 a vocational school was established there for the education of Batak youth. By 1922 Pendeta Mulia Nainggolan was assigned to Batavia (Djakarta) by Batak Zending in response to a request from Bataks there. In 1912 Pendeta Josia Hutabarat began a congregation in Medan for the growing number of urban Bataks there. Later, churches developed in other cities of Indonesia and Southeast Asia wherever Bataks settled.

Batak evangelism among the Sakai or Senoi aboriginal peo-

---

3 Peter Beyerhaus and H. Lefever, *The Responsible Church and the Foreign Mission*, p. 121.

4 Th. Müller-Krüger, *Sedjarah Geredja di Indonesia*, p. 209.

ple of Malaya was begun around 1930 by Mr. B. W. F. Napitoepoeloe, J. Pohan and M. B. A. Sihombing. The work has
centered around the Tapah, Kampar and Tanjong Malim
Districts of the Perak highlands and has been associated with
several sponsoring denominations, including the two Lutheran
churches of Malaysia. The Gospel of St. John, Luther's Catechism, One Hundred Hymns and a pamphlet entitled "The
Way of Salvation" have been translated into the Senoi language and a network of preaching points has been established. By 1958 there were said to be 1,000 converts among
the Senoi and in December, 1963, alone there were 253 Senoi
baptized in Batu Gajah and Behrang. In 1950 Mr. Napitoepoeloe studied in India and was ordained by Bishop Sandegren before returning to Malaya as a pastor of the HKBP to
work among the Senoi. The circumstances surrounding Napitoepoeloe's death in Tapah, Perak, in 1960 are still unclear;
he may have been murdered. The evangelization of aborigi-
nals in Malaya has always been a controversial and sensitive
issue, and Napitoepoeloe in his zeal found considerable opposition. In October, 1962, the Batak Senoi work was placed
under the HKBP congregation in Singapore and supported
by the Lutheran Conference in Malaya.[5]

At the present time the work is led by Mr. Sihombing, who
supervises evangelism while preaching in the villages on a
weekly rotation system, making regular reports to the HKBP
in Sumatra. Mr. Sihombing is accompanied by three assistants
who live in outlying villages providing leadership and con-
ducting services.[6]

Money for sending evangelists was gathered at an annual
mission festival following the fall harvest. The harvest festival,
which had been popular in pre-Christian Batak society as a
ceremony of traditional religion, was taken over by the church

---

[5] Duain W. Vierow, *A History of Lutheranism in Western Malaysia and
Singapore*, revised for publication from a thesis presented to the Faculty
of Graduate Studies, Lutheran School of Theology at Chicago, LCA/
BWM, 1968.

[6] "Special Report: Ministry to Aborigines," *World Encounter*, October,
1937, pp. 33-34.

as an opportunity for Bataks to show their gratitude and share their harvest. Funds collected by the mission festival were used to help congregations isolated in non-Christian areas of Atjeh or Minangkabau or otherwise located in impoverished regions.

The impact of missionary effort was not limited to the Batak Zending organization. In the last fifty years large numbers of Bataks migrated out of Tapanuli. As Batak Christians migrated to other parts of Indonesia they brought their faith with them. Their kinship ties with relatives back in Batakland were maintained both by their ethnic and religious loyalties. As many of these voluntary expatriates secured positions of authority throughout Indonesia, they were able to further the welfare of later migrants and helped the spread of Christianity throughout the Batak diaspora.

Merle Davis reported to the 1938 Madras Conference that seven thousand Christian Bataks were then living in Atjeh and another seven thousand among the Karo Bataks, with an estimated ten thousand scattered throughout southern Tapanuli and as many as thirty-five thousand in the eastern coastal residency of Sumatra.[7] These migrants were able to evangelize Batak communities in such Muslim regions as Atjeh, where missionaries were not allowed to settle. Motivated by growing economic pressure, a rapidly expanding population, and the fragmentation of ancestral farms, thousands of Bataks have chosen to pioneer in new areas of Sumatra.

Traveling individually, in families, or in colonies, this migration has had virtually no outside financial help, encouragement, or organized guidance. Sometimes groups of one to six families would journey to a distant region on the mere rumor that good land was available, and if word came back that the rumor was true, communities of from fifty to four hundred families would spring up. Several such colonies have been established in the Angkola-Mandailing regions, which had proven almost impervious to missionary efforts. The new arrivals were eagerly welcomed in such places as Batavia

---

7 Merle Davis, *The Economic Basis of the Church*, V, 445-46.

(Djakarta), where the Batak congregation of six hundred members would send a delegation to meet every incoming steamer from Sumatra and welcome new arrivals into the religious and social activities of the Batak community.

> It is commonly said that where you find one Christian Batak there is a man who talks about his faith; where there are two there is a prayer meeting; where there are three you find a church — and with four a choir. The little congregation of twenty Bataks in New York City supports this saying.[8]

The Batak migrants to Singapore formed prayer meetings in 1937 under the leadership of Mr. R. L. Tobing which developed into the "Batak Bible Fellowship" the following year. On June 9, 1940, the Bible Fellowship affiliated with the HKBP and was called the "Huria Kristen Batak Protestant Singapore." During the Japanese occupation, when Mr. R. L. Tobing returned to Sumatra, the group nearly died out, to be revived in 1946 under the capable leadership of Mr. E. Toruan. Mr. Toruan was ordained as Voorganger (Deacon) by the HKBP pendeta Sianturi from Palembang in 1948. Pendeta Dj. Siahaan from the HKBP served this congregation from 1952-59 but it is now being served by Mr. Toruan. The congregation continues to meet at the Tamil Methodist Church at 14 Short Street, Singapore.[9]

Batak converts were hungry for information about their new faith. By 1878 Nommensen had translated the New Testament into Toba Batak, using both romanized and old Batak script. In 1879 Missionary Schreiber had translated the New Testament into the Angkola dialect, and by 1894 Johannsen had translated the Old Testament into Toba Batak. A deaconess with the RMG also mentioned the work of Mr. Prudy, the Bible Society's colporteur, who traveled throughout Batakland in the 1890s, selling Scriptures and tracts at the village markets.[10] Numerous Bible stories, hymns, and tracts, including Bunyan's *Pilgrim's Progress*, were translated into Batak.

---

8 *Ibid.,* pp. 449-50.

9 Vierow, *op. cit.,* p. 103.

10 Hester Needham, *God First: Hester Needham's Work in Sumatra,* p. 62.

Other school materials, exposition books on the Bible, and the church magazine *Immanuel* were first published in 1890. Among the many other books that have been translated are von Bogatsky's book of devotions, a Children's Bible by Annie de Vries, and a quantity of hymns. The publication of literature has continued to be an important factor in evangelization by Batak churches.

Since the RMG was unable to evangelize all the Batak regions of Sumatra, they had no objection to other missionary societies moving into the outskirts of Batakland. Other mission groups soon became interested in the Bataks, with the Netherlands Mission Society (NZG), the Methodist Episcopal Church, the Seventh-day Adventists, and the Salvation Army in the lead. By 1939 the NZG had about four thousand Christians and thirty-three churches, mostly in Karoland. The Methodists then had two thousand five hundred members, many of whom were Batak, and provided schools for about two thousand pupils.[11]

The Dutch government was careful to regulate the boundaries of mission fields and churches in the Indies. While a foreigner could have permission to live anywhere in the Indies, a special permit was required to preach in any given locality. In the strong Muslim southern provinces of Batakland it was said that "missionaries are like a thorn in the flesh of the Government officials."[12] The government was always afraid that the missionaries would cause an uprising among the Muslims. The Dutch government began a policy in 1888 that did not refuse missionaries permission to work but protected the government in case a disturbance should arise. Should the missionaries' request be granted, it would carry certain restrictions; and if those restrictions were not observed, "then residence in the Indies would be refused [them], whereby the possibility of settling elsewhere in the interior would also be automatically shut out."[13] The Dutch government influenced

11 Alexander McLeish, *Sabang to Balikpapan* (London: World Dominion, 1939), p. 6.

12 Needham, *op. cit.*, p. 227.

13 E. S. De Klerck, *History of the Netherlands East Indies* (Rotterdam: W. L. & J. Brusse, 1938), II, 390.

formation of later churches by defining comity boundaries according to ethnic and linguistic perimeters. The Dutch government apparently felt that if missionary organizations could be confined to work within ethnically homogeneous cultures there would be less social conflict and competition.

The strongest source of opposition was Islam. Although all Bataks continued to observe adat obligations as a common ground for communication of ideas, the subject of Islam or Christianity was avoided by mutual agreement. Conversion to Islam often meant renouncing one's Batak identity and becoming Malay, while the Christians retained their Batak adat and ethnic identity. The missionaries and Batak Christian colonists in Muslim territories were often subjected to extreme social ostracism, causing some Bataks to leave the church for Islam.[14] The church has been very cautious toward Islam in Indonesia, in spite of guaranteed religious freedom. The Christian/Islam conflict has been a continual source of smoldering violence in Indonesia, like the semiactive volcanoes abounding in that country. The cautious harmony between these two religions in recent years has been the result of much hard work and dedication from both sides.

2. CHURCH, SCHOOL, AND HOSPITAL

With Christianity, three alien realities were introduced into Batakland.[15] The first of these was the church. Nommensen did not try at first to convert whole tribes but began with individuals. Conversion tended to break down homogeneous kinship groups and introduce a new kind of loyalty to an overarching institution that extended beyond both the family and the whole Batak community. The social identity of villages and kinship groups was later accommodated by the church, while the parbaringan organization and bius celebration were supplanted by the church organization. In 1880 Nommensen went to Europe to discuss the setting up of church regulations with the RMG according to the needs of

---

14 Hendrik Kraemer, *From Mission Field to Independent Church*, pp. 60-61.

15 Walter Freytag, *Spiritual Revolution in the East*, pp. 79ff.

the Bataks. The aim was to design a set of regulations sensitive to the peculiarities of the Batak setting.

According to this original set of regulations, those who held positions of authority in the Batak community before their conversion were given certain special, privileged responsibilities in the church. Schoolteachers were assigned to congregations in the same way as pendeta, both supported by the local congregation whenever possible. The regulations set up conferences for elders, teachers, and pendeta. District conferences were to be held two times a year, and Synod was scheduled for at least once a year. Alongside this structure a working committee made up of three missionaries was established to supervise the indigenous workers. The regulations borrowed both from foreign and indigenous models. Later, when Ephorus J. Sihombing was asked, "From which church did you model your Church Order? Which church is the HKBP?" he replied, "The HKBP is the HKBP!"[16]

After considerable study and adaptation, a third set of church regulations was validated in 1930, when the Huria Kristen Batak Protestant (HKBP) was organized and constituted as a legally independent church. These church regulations, designed under the direction of Dr. Johannes Warneck, introduced church councils that took over some of the financial administration from missionaries and were made responsible for the congregational welfare.[17] The 1930 regulations were to remain unchanged for ten years and then be reviewed for possible modification. Later modifications of 1940 and 1950 were radically changed in the church regulations of 1962 in which the Kerk Bestuur replaced the previous organization of district synods and delegates to the Great Synod were drawn from each ressort, similar to the presbytery in Reformed tradition.

As the polity of the HKBP developed it retained dual foci of congregational and episcopal authority. Representation

16 Ds. A. Silitonga, "Huria Kristen Batak Protestant Selajang Padang," Oikumene, Geredja dan Masjarakat di Indonesia (Djakarta: Badan Penerbit Kristen, 1965), pp. 66f.

17 Johannes Keuning, The Toba Batak, Formerly and Now, p. 15.

was based on each autonomous congregation through the district up to the Great Synod. But at the same time, decision-making power was directed by the church hierarchy through the office of Ephorus, Kerk Bestuur, praeses, and pendeta down to the individual congregation. Each congregation is a member of a ressort under the leadership of an ordained pendeta. These ressorts are formed into districts under the leadership of an ordained pendeta in the office of praeses. Each district had its own Synod, but the controlling body of the church was the Great Synod made up of delegates from each district and led by the Ephorus. The Kerk Bestuur, or working committee of the HKBP, is chosen by Synod delegates throughout the church, representing pendeta, teachers, elders, and laity so that while each individual congregation has representative authority, the church leaders have a parallel line of authority to interpret the regulations. For example, the Ephorus has power to transfer each pendeta from one post to another, working together with the Kerk Bestuur, and the power to appoint each pendeta to a position of authority within the hierarchy. The episcopal characteristic of central-ization, inherited from earlier patterns of missionary work, has been the cause of some dissension in the HKBP during recent years.

A variety of methods were used to secure financial resources. Spiritual, moral, and social pressure was exerted on those church members who were arrears in their payments. This might involve posting their names in the church, reading their names from the pulpit, or, if they fell a year behind, refusing them the services of the church in baptism or marriage. On occasion, individual churches have issued bonds to the Chris-tian community. Also a small building tax has been levied on Christian property owners in addition to their annual con-tributions. Special gifts of thanksgiving are taken at each church festival and two offerings are collected at services. Auctions are another popular form of fund-raising, with the most common called, for some unknown reason, an "American auction." All bids are carefully recorded and the bidder is expected to pay the difference between the previous bid and his own, whether he makes the last bid or not. These bazaars are widely practiced as much for reasons of fellowship as finance.

A number of different worship forms were used in the HKBP. Before the people went to their daily work it was common to assemble in the church for a short service, with a similar assembly in the evenings. In the morning and at evening the church bell would ring the angelus and each Christian would observe a moment of silent prayer. Hester Needham, a deaconess with the HKBP in the 1890s, reported that after Sunday sermons Missionary Johannsen would walk up and down the aisle "questioning the people so as to make them understand."[18] Nommensen gives an interesting description of his own church services.

> On Sunday we gather together early after eating and consider with one another a section of the Bible as long as we can until we are disturbed by others. There is no sermon, but instead an edifying hour where each may speak. With song and prayer begun and ended. Afterward the baptized and the catechumens go together into some village in order to speak with younger companions about their soul's salvation.[19]

Gradually the service assumed a uniform shape. The Scripture and part of the liturgy are read by an elder, with a short exposition of the text given at each service. It used to be true that a different Bible verse would be memorized each Sunday, with persons chosen at random asked to repeat the verse learned the previous Sunday. Celebration of Holy Communion is limited to twice a year, following patterns of worship introduced by missionaries.

The annual sunrise service throughout Batakland on Easter Sunday provides an example of maintaining respect for the ancestors in a context of Christian worship. The Saturday before Easter is spent cleaning up cemeteries, and in Medan, where I attended such a service, in 1964, the families were already beginning to gather at the cemetery by midnight. As each family gathered around the graves of departed mem-

---

18 Needham, *op. cit.*, p. 33.
19 Lehman, *Gottes Volk im vielen Ländern*, p. 137.

bers their torches and lanterns illuminated the whole area. Their picnic lunches were spread out between grave stones as each family gathered in happy celebration in this incongruous setting. Each family held its own private services before dawn, officiated by the senior family member with hymns, prayer, and devotional. At dawn the families assembled into their respective congregations and the air was filled with the sound of Christian hymns accompanied by brass bands and trumpets. The overwhelming impression was one of joyful celebration in sharp contrast to the fearful specter ancestors presented through traditional religion. The entire family, living and dead, were present in a context of worship. It was a memorial to the dead and a reminder to the living of Christ's resurrection, which dispelled any power or fear of death among participants. In 1963 I attended a similar service in the small village of Parapat, which was just as exquisite in its simplicity as the Medan service in its splendor.

Other influences incorporated from the traditional religion or mission-field era have seemed to obstruct the gospel. First there was the requirement that the missionaries would have to be present whenever Holy Communion was to be celebrated. The missionary was considered to possess extraordinary powers which like mana were extended to his robes, Bibles, chalice, and communion plate. In the order of service manual, written in 1904 by missionaries Jung and Steinsiek, there were two kinds of liturgy for a Sunday service: one for services led by an ordained *domine* or missionary, and one for the service led by an elder or lay-preacher. The following elements did not occur in the second liturgy: first, the votum and introit; second, the promise of forgiveness of sins, meaning that an elder or teacher could not say the sentence, "Let us hear the promise concerning the forgiveness of sins"; third, the benediction at the end of the service.[20] This status distinction between clergy and laity, begun by the missionaries, has been continued into the present day. Only the

---

[20] Andar Lumbantobing, "Sahala of a Medicine Man and a Theological Graduate," *South East Asia Journal of Theology*, January, 1963, p. 10.

pendeta is allowed to wear a robe, required for the administration of sacraments, as a sign of special authority.

The conversion of whole villages and clan groups as social
units served to preserve the kinship hierarchy, shaping the
church organization along familiar lines. During the early
Dutch administration of Tapanuli, some missionaries accepted civil responsibilities in addition to mission work.
The contiguity of ecclesiastical and civil order caused par-
tial fusion of the Christian and civil community encouraging
legalistic formalism. "The *aturan* (regulation) was given un-
due authority, and the young Church was not completely
successful in asserting her spiritual nature when challenged
by nationalism."[21]

At the "Church and Society" DGI Conference at Parapat
in 1967 M. L. Siagian cited four instances of conflict between
adat-sanctioned traditions and Christian responsibility. The
first problem involved *kawin lari* (eloping) to avoid the
expensive formalities of a church wedding. This increasingly
popular practice is particularly common in larger cities with
an estimated 80 percent of the couples in Medan choosing
to elope. The expensive adat ceremonies that must accompany
a church wedding include decorations, clothes, large amounts
of food, and gifts for the many guests who must be invited.
Only the very wealthy or those willing to go deep into debt
can afford a proper church wedding. It is far less expensive
to have a simple kawin lari ceremony conducted by a church
elder and avoid the expensive festivities associated with a
pendeta-officiated church wedding. All that is legally required
is that the marriage be registered with the government, while
social requirements are usually satisfied by a simple ceremony
where relatives, close friends, and neighbors are invited.

Another problem is that of *warisan* (inheritance rights).
In Tapanuli women do not have equal inheritance rights
with men. A court decision in 1961 has recognized equal rights
among children of the deceased, but among the Karo, for
example, a woman has to employ an expert on inheritance

21 Beyerhaus, *op. cit.,* p. 146.

rights at considerable expense to press her claim. Until recently, a childless widow had no inheritance rights. Following a 1960 court decision the widow is allowed a portion of her dead husband's inheritance to keep until she either dies or remarries.

A third problem concerns the many *tugu* (ancestral monuments) that have been erected throughout Batakland. The practice of erecting large concrete representations of marga founders has become particularly popular the last few years. Many marga have erected such monuments in the name of carrying out the commandment "to honor thy father and mother," while solidifying loyalties to the clan. Besides costing millions of *rupiah* these monuments have led Bataks to revive ancient practices of traditional religion, causing many disturbances in the Batak community. It is not infrequent for a childless wife to bring an offering to the monument of her marga ancestor asking his help in securing children. The adat festivities inaugurating new monuments have sometimes led to inter-marga quarrels so violent that the army has been called out to restore order. The Bataks have a proverb: "Djadi Tugu, dongan mardugu!" (Erect a Tugu and brothers will quarrel).

A fourth area of conflict involves the *gondang* or traditional Batak music accompanying any large social gathering or feast. The gondang has been justified as an attempt to revive and nurture Batak traditions as part of the general cultural revival of Indonesian traditions, although these ancient traditions throughout Indonesia have been closely related to regional religious practices. In the heat of celebration, accompanied by the hypnotic rhythm of the gondang gongs, you will sometimes hear the name of the High God, Ompunta Debata Muladjadi Nabolon. The church is concerned about this revival of traditional religion. Accompanying the gondang there is traditional dancing where, under traditional religion, Bataks sought to communicate with ancestral spirits. Since these dances and music are part of Batak traditions it is no mistake to preserve them and practice them as long as that practice is clearly separated from traditional religion.

There is still no contemporary application of traditional Batak music to the liturgy of Christian worship. The gondang have never been used in a church service, and perhaps the time is still not ripe for such an application.

The second alien reality Christianity introduced was medical science. In 1934 Walter Freytag estimated that a hundred thousand persons were being treated annually at Tarutung and Balige, along with four hundred to five hundred lepers and large numbers of blind and crippled Bataks who were being attended by trained nurses, midwives, and foreign doctors.[22] Formerly, the social welfare of the community was regulated by the adat, where social sanctions assured the Batak that he would be cared for by his kinship group. As the adat began to weaken it became necessary to supplement the adat and organize programs of social service. The work of the church to eliminate slavery and usury and to establish medical care laid the basis for a social program. These services often provided a bridge between the missionary and the doubtful, suspicious Batak. Lepers were formerly thrown out of their villages, or sometimes their houses were burned down around them. The first dormitory for care and treatment of lepers was opened near a mineral hot spring in Angkola. Another very large dormitory was later erected near Lake Toba called Huta Salem (Peace Village) for the care and treatment of lepers. Hundreds of lepers were treated and many of them were able to return to society.

Another dormitory called Hephata was opened up near Huta Salem for the blind and disabled. This dormitory also provided training for those people to read and learn a trade. There was also the problem of orphans. It had not been necessary to provide care for orphans as long as the adat was strong. When social conditions worsened following the Second World War, the church became concerned about the welfare of orphans and opened a dormitory and training school near Pematang Siantar in 1955. This work and other activities have flourished under the courageous leadership of Lucius Siahaan, now directing social services in the HKBP,

---

22 Freytag, *op. cit.*, p. 79.

with an efficient organizational network on the congregational and regional levels.

A hospital was opened at the church headquarters in Pearadja on June 2, 1900, and was later moved to Tarutung in 1928. Later a hospital was established at Balige, with medical clinics set up in Samosir and throughout Batakland. These hospitals were later confiscated by the Japanese and, except for the hospital at Balige which was returned to the HKBP in 1955, are still under government control. Hospital work gave many Christian youth the opportunity to study and become medical technicians, midwives, as well as nurses and doctors.

The third alien reality introduced to Batak society came through the educational institutions of the church. Where formerly only a chosen few were instructed in the wisdom of the datu and learning was associated with magical science as a venerated source of power, now the church began to lay the foundation of public education. In pre-Christian society it was not the family who exerted a molding educational influence on the youth but the whole clan who brought up the children. The Batak saw education as the key to power for the missionary and perhaps for himself as well. Education provided positions of power. Ignorance was associated with weakness. "The European has education, that is why he could conquer us, so thinks the heathen, for the European is less robust physically than we."[23]

The original purpose of education was to enable the new converts better to understand the gospel, and theological subjects dominated the curriculum. "The congregation assembled in worship is the core of Church education."[24] Education trained converts for baptism and confirmation into the church, with all Christian children as early as 1910 required to attend confirmation class for one or two years of instruction in Bible history and the Catechism. In 1899 Hester Need-

---

[23] Gottfried Simon, *Progress and Arrest of Islam in Sumatra*, p. 44.

[24] Andar Lumbantobing, "Christian Education in the Batak Church," *Lutheran World*, II (Autumn, 1955), 295f.

ham began a Bible school for women at Silindung and Sister Lisette Diemann began a similar school in the Toba area.

When the Dutch annexed Batak territory they decided to subsidize the system of mission schools begun by the RMG. In order to receive government subsidy a school had to enroll a minimum of thirty children and be located at least four kilometers from any neighboring school. There was a system of three- to five-year folk schools throughout the land where elementary education was given by a mission teacher, who also led the congregation on Sundays. There were, moreover, a few Hollands Inlandse Schools and at Tarutung a school for more advanced elementary education (Meer Uitgebreid Lager Onderwijs), all in the hands of the mission. The government also established several secular schools, with optional religious instruction and with Malay as a subject, where the curriculum was designed toward preparation for eventual government positions. Generally, however, it was the church that wished to encourage higher education rather than the government. Most of the church schools continued through the fifth and sixth grades, while government public schools stopped at the third grade. The RMG also operated a large industrial school at Laguboti on Lake Toba, which received no government or mission subsidy beyond the salary of its director and showed an annual profit by contracting outside work.

The first theological training school was opened at Prau Sorat in 1868, only six years after the first congregation was formed, but closed in 1873. In 1877 a new school was established in Pansurnapitu, admitting students who had completed a five-year elementary school course. Under the direction of missionaries Dr. A. Schreiber and Leipoldt this school provided three courses for the education of evangelists. In 1883 the first regular theological school was opened for the training of pastors alongside the seminary. Due to space limitations the Sekola Pendeta (Pastors' School) was moved to Sipoholon from Pansurnapitu in 1901. The Sekola Pendeta accepted graduates from the teachers' school for further training as pendeta.

The candidate for "school teacher and gospel preacher" first had to complete five years of primary study, and after two years at the training school he would take the government examination for a teacher's certificate. Then followed two more years of study to prepare him for pastoral work in the congregation. The teacher-preacher was vested with the dual authority of the church and Department of Education. If he wished to qualify for ordination he would have to work successfully for about ten years in a congregation and then return for two more years of theological training. These men were responsible for an incredible amount of work in the congregations.

> The Teacher-Preacher is vested with dual authority of the Great Synod and the Department of Education. In a large community assisted by one or more paid assistants, he devotes himself to his school from seven to one o'clock six days a week and two evenings a week he teaches confirmation classes; on two afternoons he trains his presbyters in preaching and methods of parish work; on another afternoon he again meets his presbyters to receive reports and discuss with them their problems in parish work; on three evenings a week he visits the sick and the neediest families. He spends one hour a week with the young men's group, one hour with the teachers of the Sunday School and one afternoon each week he trains the church choir. On Sundays he preaches and supervises the Sunday School in the morning and in the afternoon he attends the young people's meeting and leads the Bible study and singing.[25]

It was difficult to secure admission to the seminary at Sipoholon, for only about 10 percent of the candidates were accepted. The cost of the first two years was covered by the government and subsequent years by the family of the student. In 1934 another seminary was established near Batavia (Djakarta) at Buitenzorg, established by the Indian church, the Allied Missionary Societies, the Basel Mission, and the RMG. P. T. Sarumpaet, K. Sitompul, T. Sihombing, and O. Sihotang were enrolled in the first year from the HKBP. The objective was to convey knowledge of Western

---

25 Davis, *op. cit.,* pp. 174-75.

theology over a six-year course, provide an adequate personal library, and train students as future leaders in the sending churches.[26] Each of the men sent from the HKBP have held and continue to hold positions of highest authority not only in the HKBP but LWF and WCC as well. T. S. Sihombing is serving as Ephorus of the HKBP and is active in the WCC; K. Sitompul holds positions of authority in the LWF and Indonesian Council of Churches as well as the HKBP; and Sarumpaet is now Chief of Protestant Chaplains for the Indonesian Armed Forces.

3. HAMADJUON BATAK (BATAK PROGRESSIVISM)

The key word in Batak society became *hamadjuon* (progress), and missionaries reported with dismay the materialistic enthusiasm for advancement among the Batak people. On the one hand the Batak retained a traditionally fatalistic attitude that "God has made me as I am and He must use me as I am made." On the other hand Christianity brought a new "self consciousness" to the Batak people. As a young Batak editor explained: "Christianity's message of the equality of all men before God — you notice that I emphasize 'before God' — has freed us from an oppressive inferiority complex and has given us the power as a nation of rising to higher things."[27] Every influence was evaluated according to its contribution toward progress.

Progress and development toward nation- and church-building encountered the problem of achieving dynamic and organizational efficiency without abandoning important elements of the old traditions. General T. B. Simatupang, who grew up in Tarutung, describes Christian service as the key factor in this transition, expanding the notion of service beyond helping needy persons into the wider struggle for political, social, and economic justice. Otherwise, Simatupang warns, Christian youth who become active in movements working toward social, economic, and political justice outside

---

26 Johannes Rauws, H. Kraemer, F. J. F. van Hasselt, and N. A. C. Slatemaker de Bruine, *The Netherlands Indies,* pp. 149f.

27 Freytag, *op. cit.,* p. 86.

the church will find many of the church teachings irrelevant. General Simatupang cites his own experiences in Batakland as an example.

> At a certain period in my life, I was caught up in the nation-alist struggle for independence. It was as if a world with new perspective and values was opened up, providing a new mean-ing and direction to life. Membership in the Church, which basically continued the old routine, became less and less sig-nificant in the face of the ideals of freedom, justice, pros-perity for all, equality and fraternity. Later on, I realized that the Church was not prepared theologically and otherwise to respond to the tremendous and rapid changes in the society.[28]

The Bataks wanted more than conversion to Christianity. They wanted an improved material existence and the op-portunity to break out of the limitations imposed by tradi-tional isolationism. Many times the missionary demanded a spiritual discipline that was beyond the Batak's desire and human capability. As early as the time of van der Tuuk, who was not prone to moralizing, there was a complaint against the matter-of-fact, materialistic greed of the Bataks. "The only things which interested them in their first con-tacts with the Gospel were increased wealth, prestige and power. If the Gospel could bring them these things, they were ready to listen, if not they were not."[29] The missionaries did bring prestige and power, and Christianity strengthened their self-conscious identity as Bataks. Even where anti-Euro-pean influences led some to abandon the mission, the church would remain as something necessary, something they took for granted as part of the new age they were entering.

The Dutch built a new road through the middle of Batak-land in 1919, laying the region open to nonmissionary West-ern influences. A missionary reported that fitting electric lights into the hospital had made a greater impression on the Bataks than his sermons. Dr. Winkler at the church hospital

---

28 T. B. Simatupang, "Life in Christ—Called to Service and Nation-Building," in Soritua A. E. Nababan, *Christ The Life,* p. 68.

29 Kraemer, *op. cit.,* p. 44.

warned the Barmen RMG headquarters that this new influence would have an inevitable effect on the health and morality of the region, with the coming of venereal disease and
"other difficulties of mind and body" forcing themselves on
the Bataks.[30] The forces of nationalism, independence, and
hamadjuon proved much more contagious than venereal
disease.

Missionaries valued the isolation of Batakland and were
generally opposed to emigration toward the modernized
coastal regions.[31] The younger Bataks were, however, especially attracted to the revolutionary awakening throughout
Asia. The mission school education itself kindled these pro-
gressive tendencies in their view of economic life and social
attitudes. To emulate European education and material
wealth and attain higher social prestige became an expression of hamadjuon for the modern Batak.

It was not easy for the Christian Batak to live in a city
such as Medan during the first part of the twentieth century.
They were under the authoritarian control of an Islamic
Sultan and were regarded as unbelievers (kafir) and unclean
(nadjis), pig eaters and cannibals, segregated to restricted
areas of the city, and limited in their opportunities for employment. "If Christian grace was said in a public restaurant,
the Bataks were requested to leave. Stones and dirt were
thrown against the roofs of the private homes in which they
held church services."[32] In response to this pressure many of
the Bataks along the coast accepted Islam; others dropped
their Batak clan names, learned to speak Malay, and identified themselves with the coastal Malays. The larger proportion would disguise rather than renounce their Batak identity,
posing as Malays but practicing their religion in secret, and
return to the villages for adat ceremonies. When the Batak
community in Medan grew to sufficient size, many of these

30 Müller-Krüger, op. cit., p. 191.

31 W. F. Wertheim, Indonesian Society in Transition (Bandung: Sumur
Bandung, 1956), pp. 186f. Also note Kraemer, op. cit., p. 67.

32 Edward M. Bruner, "Urbanization and Ethnic Identity in North
Sumatra," American Anthropologist, LXIII (1961), 511.

Bataks sought to reestablish contact with their clan and organized into numerous ceremonial and recreational associations.

The attraction of hamadjuon was especially strong among the youth. The orderly restrictions adat had placed on former generations did not harmonize with rapid social change in Batakland. There were now ways to rise in status by circumventing the restrictive adat hierarchy and gain power, wealth, or influence. It was difficult to enforce kinship obligations, and clan responsibilities were left unfulfilled. Traditionally, child rearing had followed permissive lines for fear of incurring the displeasure of the child's tondi. "The child rules the home. It does not know obedience in the European sense; whatever enters its head must be carried out."[33] Therefore it was only when a youth reached marriageable age that the full restrictive forces of adat fell on him, and it was at that point that many Batak youth rebelled.

The traditional guidelines of pre-Christian Batak culture that had been rejected by parents or grandparents were no longer able to serve youth as a guide, but probably neither had the youth made any personal decision for Christianity as their parents and grandparents had done. In Tapanuli the youth often tended to be indifferent or hypercritical toward their faith. Davis tells of the youth in a Tarutung church, often critical of the pendeta for being less educated than they, who would "occasionally take notes during the sermon and freely praise or disparage the preaching, sending in their criticism to the minister."[34]

Many of the young men would go to Java to complete their education and encounter "the materialistic and reactionary influences of city life," to be "infected" by nationalism, the cinema, the newspaper, and venereal disease. The Great Synod passed a regulation that every young man who had been in Java must present a certificate of good health before he could be married in the church.[35] There was active

33 Andar Lumbantobing, "Christian Education in the Batak Church," *op. cit.,* p. 293.
34 Davis, *op. cit.,* p. 442.

opposition by many families in Batakland toward these youth who wished to visit the outside world, as one Batak pendeta recounts:

> When I was a boy in Tapanuli and left to study in Singapore, walking the long way down to the coast, the women in the family moaned and cried, fearing that I would fall off the earth and never come back. Today, the women will moan and cry if a son does not have ambition and does not want to leave the huta and go into business or to school.[36]

In the 1930s the HKBP organized a youth movement with two branches. One branch was among the Batak youth studying in Java and another among those in Batakland itself. The movement published its own newspaper, organized annual conferences, and sponsored evangelistic meetings. Missionary E. Verwiebe was sent out by the YMCA in Germany to assist with the work among Batak youth, but within a few years he was forced to give up his work for lack of funds. Going from village to village he organized the young people for discussion and debate. "He invited those who were longing for a new life to attend groups for Bible Study; he arranged conferences and meetings to discuss the questions of our day, thus leading the minds of the young generation into the light of Christ."[37]

4. THE SECOND WORLD WAR

On May 10, 1940, when the Nazi armies entered the Netherlands, all sixty German missionaries, including wives and children, doctors and deaconesses who worked in the HKBP, were assembled at 6:00 A.M. by the Dutch for internment. The leadership was suddenly withdrawn throughout the church, the seminary, hospitals, leprosarium, Huta Salem, and Hephata. The reactions among Bataks varied. For some, when the German missionaries were interned, this caused little

---

35 E. Verwiebe, "Youth Problem in the Batak Church in Sumatra," *International Review of Missions*, April, 1938, p. 210.

36 Clark E. Cunningham, *The Postwar Migration of the Toba-Bataks to East Sumatra*, p. 78.

37 Lehman, *op. cit.*, p. 144.

commotion. "One may almost say that it provided a sense
of relief among the Batak."[38] Calling an emergency Synod
meeting in July, 1940, the HKBP filled the vacant posts with
Bataks, electing Pendeta K. Sirait to be Ephorus. The hospitals and schools, which had been partly subsidized by the
government, were taken over by the Commisie voor Rechts-
verkeer in Oorlogstijd; and the government recognized a
Dutch-led organization called the Batak Nias Zending to
assume responsibility for German work.

The three Dutch missionaries who headed the BNZ gave
their full consent to the election of a Batak Ephorus, but dis-
agreed with the HKBP on many other points. The BNZ
prevailed on the Dutch government to turn all schools and
buildings over to their organization rather than the HKBP
and further recommended that the teachers in church schools
were to receive their salaries from the government through
the BNZ, which would then control the activities of the
school. While the Dutch missionaries realized that their staff
was insufficient to continue the work of German missionaries
as before and while they looked forward to the formation
of an indigenous Batak church, they felt this transition should
be gradual and thus avoid administrative difficulties. The
HKBP, however, decided that "the missionaries are now to
be called, following the example of East Java, 'church visitors,' and this is defined by the Bataks to mean, 'they have
admission to all our meetings, our homes, and our churches;
they are always welcome.'" The significance of this decision
was not lost on the Dutch missionary who commented that
"the European missionaries have wholly lost their central
position and real power for them has not been preserved."[39]

Offers of assistance from the BNZ were rejected by the
HKBP for several reasons. First, the BNZ would not recognize many of the leaders chosen by the HKBP at their emergency Great Synod. Second, the BNZ sought to divide the

---

[38] *Ibid.;* also see "Survey of European War and Missions," *International
Review of Missions,* XXX (1941), 26f.

[39] "Survey of European War and Missions," *International Review of
Missions,* XXX (1941), 26-27.

church in the Angkola region from the rest of the HKBP. Third, the congregational teachers were to become civil servants, under the control of the Dutch government. Fourth, the hospitals and clinics were to be nationalized. Many doubted that the HKBP would be able to survive independently. One Dutch missionary in the BNZ compared the HKBP to a train of cars that have broken free from their engine, which can coast for awhile but must finally come to a halt.[40]

Over five hundred schools were placed under the care of Dutch missionaries, who functioned as administrators with far-reaching authority. The preacher-teachers no longer felt obligated to serve their local congregations, and, while a few remained out of loyalty, most of them no longer wished to be burdened with parish work. Many of them in fact feared the schools might be returned to the church, in which case their responsibilities would be increased and their salaries decreased. The church was therefore forced to find laymen, who were usually elders without theological training, to fill the vacancies.[41]

The estrangement between church and school was deepened during the Japanese occupation of Indonesia. The Japanese brought their own ideas and teachers, consuming the time of the youth and directing all their attention and energy toward these new ideas. Although Christian instruction was not prohibited by the Japanese, there was a strong attempt to spread the religious and cultural heritage of Japan. "Many a teacher and preacher met a martyr's death, yet even so, it is regrettable that no determined and unanimous 'No!' was uttered."[42] One of the Japanese officers spoke to the leaders of the church, saying: "I will not leave Batakland before you put aside Christianity for my religion."[43] This attitude was carried out by encouraging Shinto worship, forcing

[40] Ds. P. T. Sarumpaet, "Kristus Adalah Evangelium Dalam Kesulitan," *Seratus Tahun Kekristenan Dalam Sedjarah Rakjat Batak* (Tarutung, 1961), p. 64.

[41] Andar Lumbantobing, "Christian Education in the Batak Church," *op. cit.*, pp. 292ff.

[42] *Ibid.*, p. 294.

[43] Silitonga, *op. cit.*, p. 69.

church members to work on Sundays, forbidding the singing
of hymns and teaching of Christianity in schools, while church
meetings were carefully regulated and closely observed.

As a consequence, a generation of youth grew up "which
knows so pitifully little of the Bible that even four years of
confirmation instruction in place of the present two would
not be likely to remedy the situation."[44] Equally serious was
the absence of theological training for Batak pendeta, resulting in a serious shortage of pendeta today. After the Japanese defeat came years of revolution and civil war that
further disrupted Christian teaching. In the struggle for national and regional independence, freedom demanded a total
commitment of Indonesian youth.

5. FACTORS IN RAPID BATAK CHURCH GROWTH

Several attempts have been made to describe the development of the HKBP in terms of stages or periods of development. In the 1930s Dr. E. Verwiebe, the former Ephorus of
the HKBP, suggested a four-stage structure of Batak church
growth.[45] In the first stage the patriarchal missionary had
complete control and responsibility. During the second stage
missionary-trained elders and Batak pendeta were allowed
to give their advice but the missionary retained ultimate responsibility. At the third stage, realized in the regulations
of 1930, financial responsibility was turned over to consis-
tories while the missionary retained only the right of veto.
Verwiebe finally looked forward to a fourth stage when the
missionary would be supplanted by well-trained Batak
pendeta. Equally serious was the lack of theological training
for Batak pendeta resulting in a serious shortage of pendeta.

Another approach was suggested by Dr. N. Arne Bendtz,
former LWF representative in Sumatra. He describes the
development in terms of four basic strategies.[46] The first

---

44 Andar Lumbantobing, "Christian Education in the Batak Church,"
op. cit., p. 294.

45 E. Verwiebe, "The Batak Church in Sumatra," *op. cit.*, p. 133.

46 N. Arne Bendtz, "Lutheran Strategies in World Mission," *Augustana
Theological Seminary Review*, IX, 2 (1957), 25-32.

strategy was to build a bulwark of mission stations against militant Muslims in the South. This would prevent other alien ideologies from penetrating the Batak community. Second, there was a strategic advance to the independent northern Bataklands aimed not only at individual conversions but at a whole ethnic folk church. The third strategy was to preserve the existing ethnic structure. "It was not the pagan resistance to the Christian message that was the main obstacle to the change of mind of the people, but the anchorage of the individual in his natural social life."[47] The danger that Christianity might become simply a new law, like the old adat, was met with a fourth strategy intended to deepen the spiritual understanding of the Batak community after conversion. This missionary task was best done by the Bataks themselves, who knew the country and people, spoke Batak as their native language, and did not carry the stigma of being foreigners.

Beyond descriptions of what happened among the Bataks, there is much that remains to be explained and understood. The mission arrived on the scene at the right time, when the Bataks were seeking a new way of life better suited to the problems and opportunities of modernization and Westernization than their traditional adat. This was especially the case for such Batak leaders as Radja Pontas Lumbantobing, who guided Nommensen in his early years among the Bataks. These leaders had great foresight, and without their assistance it is doubtful the mission would have made much of an impact on the Bataks. Traditionally, much credit has been given to Nommensen and his policies. His incorporation of existing leadership structures into the church organization made Christianity much more acceptable to the radjas. Nommensen depended greatly on these "guardians of the adat" with secular power, and their contribution to the rapid expansion of Christianity was substantial. "For they are heads of a lineage, of a territory comprising several villages; they constitute an example for all the men and women who recog-

---

47 *Ibid.*, p. 29.

nize them as leaders; they are the public conscience, as it were, the protectors of adat and the law."[48]

Batak churchmen inherited many leadership responsibilities in Batakland following the establishment of Christianity. A modern example of courageous leadership is Dr. J. Sihombing, who held the position of Ephorus in the HKBP for twenty years. During this difficult time during the war and revolution he demonstrated special leadership qualities in settling disputes between warring factions. The wisdom he brought to conflict situations in the church is already legendary. Although retired he continues to serve as preacher, lecturer, and author of numerous articles on the continuing effect of animistic belief among church members. He is the author of several books in Batak on church history, preaching, and pastoral care and retains several unpublished manuscripts including one on early Christian Batak biographies. At the present time he continues teaching at Nommensen Seminary. In recognition of his contribution the University of Bonn, which had granted Dr. Nommensen his honorary degree, also granted Ephorus J. Sihombing an honorary doctorate.

During the period of rapid expansion the Batak region was largely under the care of a single missionary organization, the RMG, around Lake Toba. This simplified problems of organization and direction of resources without outside competition. The financial policy of self-support, which after the First World War was pursued out of necessity, strengthened each individual congregation and prevented the development of expensive institutions. At the same time, government subsidies were available to maintain those institutions considered essential. Accommodation of Batak adat and tribal law to church discipline helped make the transition to Christianity from traditional religion, filling the old forms with new content. The unique personality of the Bataks themselves, retaining clan solidarity, pioneering new areas through colonies, and maintaining an aggressive independent

---

48 Keuning, *op. cit.*, p. 11.

36009

attitude, made them tenacious defenders of the Christian faith. Ultimately, the explanation of rapid expansion lies in the personality of the Batak people themselves.

The missionary, while playing an important role in leadership, cannot claim credit for the remarkable growth of the Batak church. After the First World War, when the numbers of missionary personnel were severely curtailed, their work was largely limited to supervision through Batak leaders in the church. Each missionary was responsible for the welfare of churches in his district, and requests for foreign financial aid were channeled through the missionary to the mission. They discovered at an early stage that affairs of church discipline and pastoral guidance on the congregational level could be most effectively implemented by the Bataks among other Bataks. "Beyond occasionally taking the service during his tours, the missionary usually does not concern himself with details of church work and seldom undertakes evangelistic preaching."[49] This is not to ignore the role of the mission or missionary, nor does it suggest that the Christianization of Batakland could have been accomplished without foreign missionary assistance. It does suggest that there are many anonymous heroes among the early Batak Christians and that the church has continued to make remarkable progress independent of missionary leadership.

In spite of the remarkable growth of the Batak church, the RMG has come under some criticism for its mission policies. Dr. Hendrik Kraemer visited the HKBP, at the request of Ephorus Dr. Johannes Warneck, in March and April, 1930. Kraemer was critical of the mission, or missionaries, for concentrating on their own aims in a paternalistic regard for the Batak people. This meant that "missions were too exclusively possessed of the desire to raise a strong Christian community and a strong Church, and did not sufficiently desire to build up a strong Christian people."[50] In the words of one Batak to Dr. Kraemer, "They are too much like officials. But what is accepted from an official is not accepted

---

49 Davis, *op. cit.*, p. 422.
50 Kraemer, *op. cit.*, p. 68.

Lincoln Christian College

from and condoned in a missionary."[51] But more seriously, he did not feel that the mission had much insight into this difficulty. He credited this largely to the fact that most of the RMG staff at that time had been in service since before the First World War and were out of touch with the changing currents of the times. Gottfried Simon, who was an RMG missionary to the Simalungun Bataks, describes the missionary's attitude toward the Batak at the beginning of the twentieth century, in the midst of the mass movement to Christianity, as that of an affectionate teacher. "He does not take advantage of his racial superiority to victimize the native, he seeks to serve him. The superior race assumes responsibility for the inferior. This is the Christian solution to the racial problem."[52] It was often easier to serve the Bataks than for the missionary to share his decision-making powers with them.

Finally, the role of the Batak layman must be emphasized as an important factor in rapid Batak church growth. Approximately 90 percent of the worship services each Sunday are led by Batak laymen as well as regular midweek devotionals in the homes. Without dedicated elders, teachers, and members who lead prayer meetings, visit the sick, and carry out responsibility for pastoral care the Batak churches would have found growth impossible.

---

[51] *Ibid.*, p. 69.
[52] Simon, *op. cit.*, p. 279.

IV

THE PLURALITY
OF BATAK CHURCHES

As the number of Batak Christians increased, so did the variety of missionary organizations and indigenous churches. Cultural differences of Batak tribes and doctrinal distinctions between missionary organizations extinguished the earlier hope for a Batak, ethnic, folk church. This chapter attempts to trace the differentiation of Batak churches leading up to the contemporary autonomous plurality of churches. The complex multiplicity of traditions, both indigenous and foreign, necessitated a broad range of strategies and approaches among these different churches.

The scarcity of materials on Batak churches other than the HKBP has led to primary dependence on a single source for the description of each church discussed in the following chapter. The description of the Simalungun church is condensed from a short, bicentenary history published by the Geredja Kristen Protestant Simalungun. The background on Methodist work is drawn largely from annual records of the Sumatra Mission Conference. Christianity among the Karo Bataks is condensed from H. Neumann's original research at the Nederlandse Zendingshogeschool, Oegstgeest Bibliotheek, Oegstgeest. The description of Roman Catholic work was supplied largely by Fr. Guido Tharappel, presently stationed at the Parapat seminary. The Pentecostal work was outlined by Missionary Howard Gering. Wherever possible, supplementary sources were used to clarify and confirm factual information.

A number of other groups and sects have also been active in evangelization among the Bataks of North Sumatra. When Missionary and Mrs. Hubert Mitchell of the "Go-Ye Fellowship," a non-denominational, fundamentalist group from Los Angeles, worked in Sumatra in 1935 they were assisted by the Batak, F. Lumbantobing, and by the end of 1935 they had made two hundred converts among the Kubus of Rawas valley and near Pageralam in South Sumatra. By 1960 the Overseas Missionary Fellowship had six missionaries in Sumatra working among established churches, especially along the west coast of Sumatra. In 1964 Mr. and Mrs. Martin Goldsmith, the first OMF missionaries to the Karo Bataks, were working in Kabandjahe and were later joined by Mr. and Mrs. Michael Dunn from England. Mrs. Goldsmith's book *Batak Miracle* (London: OMF, 1967) describes some of their experiences. The Baptists began working in North Sumatra several years ago and claim almost 100 members to date. Among the Christian groups not listed with the Indonesian Department of Religion are the Mormon missionaries and several itinerant Jehovah Witness preachers working in North Sumatra. Information on these and the many other small groups which have been active in evangelizing the Bataks is not readily available.

1. THE SIMALUNGUN CHURCH

By 1850 many of the Simalunguns had entered Islam. The Radja of Siantar was himself a Muslim. The vast majority, however, believed in a High God (Anibata latas), a Middle God (Naibata Itongah), and a Lower-world God (Naibata Itoruh). The radjas were called *naibata na taridah* (god whom we can see). The most influential of the radjas was Radja Tuan Rondahaim, who was a prominent warrior and later to become a regional hero. Tuan Rondahaim fought the

Dutch at Dolok Merawan in October, 1887, and at Bandar Padang in October, 1888, the year of his death. Five years later Christianity extended its influence into the Simalungun region.[1]

The missionaries had been working in Tapanuli forty-two years before they arrived among the Simalungun Bataks. Missionary H. Guillaume, a Dutch citizen educated in Barmen, was sent to Sumatra and loaned to the Nederlands Zendingsgenootschap in 1899 for work among the Karo. Each year when he attended the missionary conference in Tapanuli he traveled through a section of western Simalungun and gradually became acquainted with the people there. Both Missionary Guillaume and Controller van Dijk, who lived at Laguboti and visited Simalungun in 1890, encouraged Nommensen to begin work among the Simalunguns. In 1903 Nommensen appointed Missionary G. K. Simon and several evangelists from the Batak Mission Society to explore the region and evaluate the possibilities for missionary work. It was a difficult task because of intervillage hostilities and because the missionaries did not know Simalungun Batak while the Simalunguns could not speak the Toba dialect. Missionary Simon reported that Islam had a strong following in the region and it was urgently necessary to begin missionary work as soon as possible. On March 16, 1903, the RMG headquarters at Barmen confirmed this decision.

The RMG and Batak Mission Society joint strategy to evangelize the Simalungun Bataks was planned like a military campaign. First, an expedition of twenty-three evangelists and missionaries toured the Simalungun area, preaching the gospel and discussing the possibility of permanent work with village leaders. Second, all decisions were carefully discussed, securing local support from both the Dutch government and the radja in each Simalungun village. Third, there was an emphasis on education, establishing schools, and work among the youth.

1 *Tahun Indjil Kristus Di Simalungun, 2 September, 1903, to 2 September, 1963*, Pematang Siantar, Pimpinan Pusat, GKPS, 1963, p. 6. (Unless otherwise indicated, material about the Simalungun church will be drawn from this source.)

Finally, there was a carefully arranged network of mission stations and Batak evangelists spread throughout Simalungun Batakland.

As the expedition, led by Nommensen himself, traveled from village to village they were well received and the villagers welcomed their promise to return with permanent work. The group traveled as far as Pematang Siantar, on the edge of the Islamic-controlled coastal region, before turning back toward Lake Toba. A supply depot was established near Lake Toba to supply food and equipment so that the missionaries and evangelists would not be physically dependent on the Simalungun villagers. The rough terrain, lack of food, tribal warfare, and disease plagued the expedition as it would later frustrate the missionaries and evangelists.

After several further expeditions Missionary Theis became the first foreign missionary appointed to Simalungun work, stationed at Pematang Raja on September 2, 1903. The history of the Simalungun church is considered to begin from this date. Missionary Theis faced many problems. All his rice had to be carried over winding mountain paths from the supply depot at Tigaras, there was anti-Dutch hostility among the people, and rumors abounded that the radja was about to retract his promise of hospitality. Westernized Toba Batak carpenters who came to construct the mission house were accustomed to wearing trousers and protecting themselves from the sun with umbrellas, which the Simalunguns considered strange and therefore dangerous. The radja soon passed a law forbidding trousers or umbrellas and insisting on the traditional sarong dress for men. Just when the house was completed, Missionary Theis received a cable from the RMG headquarters at Barmen that he was reassigned to the island of Nias off the west coast of Sumatra! Nommensen was able to countermand the order, however, and the Pematang Raja school was soon in operation. The curriculum included reading, writing, and arithmetic as well as the study of Luther's Catechism and Bible stories. The school was held at the radja's house since the children would have been fearful of visiting the new mission station.

The adults of the village were doubtful concerning this new enterprise. There had been a rumor that the school-children, once trained, would be inducted into the Dutch army. Also, Missionary Theis was using many strange medicines to treat the sick. But gradually both the school and the medical care were accepted, and people began to arrive from far away for medical treatment. Besides Missionary Theis there was also a Batak evangelist who traveled throughout the village and surrounding areas.

The new Dutch government and Christian religion instituted many changes. As government influence increased, every person of power assumed the title of radja and, in 1908, all Spanish and English money was exchanged for Dutch currency. In conversations with the Dutch government, the missionaries requested that slavery be abolished in the region. On January 1, 1910, the government acted on this request and slavery was prohibited. The government also began to build roads connecting the villages in the region. This was accomplished through forced roadwork for thirty days a year by each adult male, except for the elderly and schoolchildren. The Simalunguns considered conscript labor as a new form of slavery, and many, although already adults, sought to enter the mission schools to evade conscription. The radjas were not united in their opposition to new roads and the Radja at Raja himself began building a road to Purba and Panei even before being directed to do so by the government.

While work among the Simalunguns went slowly, there was much to be done among the Toba Bataks who were rapidly migrating into the region. The first baptism in Simalungun did not occur until 1909 at Pematang Raja when Missionary Theis baptized several converts. Later that same year thirty-eight were baptized at Parapat. So far all the evangelists were from Tapanuli, although Missionary Theis strongly suggested that some of the local inhabitants should also be allowed to evangelize. In 1911 two Simalunguns entered the Zending-Kweekschool near Batavia, and after graduation were approved by the government to teach in schools. They were assigned as substitute teachers for the Tapanuli Bataks in the

Raja area, but Saribudolok and Parapat continued to use exclusively teachers from Tapanuli. The Toba Batak language was still used in the schools and churches. By 1928, after twenty-five years of work, there were nine hundred Simalungun Christians and thirty-one congregations.

The Simalungun situation was quite different from the earlier evangelization of Silindung and Toba. The evangelists in Simalungun worked from thirty to fifty kilometers apart, while in Silindung there had been a pendeta every five to ten kilometers. While many of the Simalunguns lived outside their villages, guarding the fields against monkeys and pigs from the jungle, the paths connecting the villages were mostly animal trails and in poor repair. It was extremely difficult to travel through the Simalungun region. The Simalunguns were conservative and unwilling to receive new ideas. When a village radja in Tapanuli entered Christianity the whole village followed him into the new religion; but not so among the Simalungun, where many families were divided with one parent accepting Christianity and the other not.

The Simalungun radjas did not care to learn about Christianity. They had several wives, while Christianity allowed only one. Also, if they entered Christianity they would have to give up their sovereign authority and accept advice from the evangelist, who was only a common villager. Although the radjas did not forbid their people from accepting Christianity, their authority over the village was somewhat undermined. From the point of view of the new convert who went to church his "radja" was the missionary, since he followed the missionary's direction. A second obstruction to evangelization was the language problem. The Toba Batak language was used in evangelization and throughout all mission schools. First the people had to learn Toba Batak, then they could learn about the gospel. The books in church and school were all written in the Toba dialect. While many Toba words resembled Simalungun, some of the words commonly used in Toba Batak have quite a different meaning in Simalungun.

On Sunday, September 3, 1928, there was a celebration at Pematang Raja commemorating twenty-five years of evangelization among the Simalunguns. Following the meeting there was a discussion concerning better ways to evangelize among the Simalunguns. Many of the group felt that not Toba but the Simalungun Batak language and personnel should be used in evangelization. Out of this discussion the Komite Na Ra Marpodah (Evangelization Committee) was established to advise evangelists. This committee issued books for church and school and the monthly magazine *Sinalsal* (Light) . The books included Luther's *Small Catechism,* Bible verses, the church liturgy, hymnals, Old and New Testament Bible stories, and devotional literature. There were three types of books for use in the schools, books on administration, and vocational literature for the general public, as well as a dictionary called *Partingkian ni hata Simalungun.*

An institute was established to be held every month for the benefit of the elders throughout congregations around Raja. This institute taught the Old and New Testament, geography of the Holy Land, and some church history. Similar institutes were held at Saribudolok and Nagori Dolok, with all three groups meeting once a year to report on progress in evangelization and study the Bible together. The group of elders was called the Kongsi Sintua (Elders Brotherhood) and was appointed to serve the new converts.

No one knows exactly how the idea of Kongsi Laita (Let's Go! Brotherhood) got started, but in 1930 it was customary for the members of the Pematang Raja congregation to meet every Sunday after church services to discuss the sermon in the coffee shops. Among the elders of the church it was also customary to spend Sunday afternoons visiting the homes of their neighbors who had not yet accepted Christianity. Gradually the number of these visitors grew and the November 15, 1931, assembly elected leaders and formulated a constitution. One principle in the original charter indicates that if a member of the Kongsi Laita continues in conversation for more than five minutes with another person he must make a witness to the gospel. At first the group was active only around Pematang Raja, but by 1936 members were being sent out to other areas of Simalungun to witness their faith. Three to seven members were sent out for a week at a time and then returned to report on their experiences. Generally they were well received, but once at Tanah Djawa they were refused permission to work since they lacked a letter from the regional pendeta, although their own pendeta at Pematang Raja had written a letter of introduction. One of the members was blind and required a child to accompany him. All labor was voluntary and no salaries were provided, with each worker expected to pay his own expenses. On the tenth anniversary of Kongsi Laita the Great Synod of the HKBP Simalungun admitted the organization into the church. After November 16, 1941, they could evangelize wherever necessary and were allowed representation at Synod.

After Missionary Simon left for Europe none of the other European missionaries worked in the Simalungun language until the arrival of H. Volmer in 1936. The other missionaries considered the Toba Batak language adequate for use among Simalunguns as well. Since the RMG was unable to help in providing a Bible in the Simalungun language, Pendeta J. Wismar Saragih began work in 1937 on a translation, beginning with the Gospel of Luke. Although he did not know Greek, he compared the texts of Dutch, Indonesian, Toba, Karo, and Angkola translations and, with the help of Missionary H. Volmer, Dr. P. Voorhoeve, and the Dutch Bible Society, he succeeded in having two thousand copies printed. Within a few weeks the printing was sold out, both because of its low price and the enthusiasm of Christians for a Simalungun translation. This provided considerable stimulus for later translations.

The Roman Catholics began work in the Pematang Raja area in 1937, distributing their literature outside the churches every Sunday. The Protestant missionary C. Gabriel issued a book called *The Way to God, According to the Teachings of the Roman Catholic Church and Protestantism.* There were five hundred copies printed and distributed among the congregations around Raja. Besides this Gabriel held meetings to clarify the teachings of the two churches. The Christians of Pematang Raja demonstrated before the Catholic Church at Sondi, demanding that no Protestant Christian should be allowed to enter the Catholic Church. After evaluating the situation, the Catholic Church at Sondi was closed and its furnishings disposed of.

In view of the differences of language, adat, and fellowship between the Simalungun and Toba Bataks it had long been recommended that besides the East Sumatra, Atjeh, and Dairi Districts, a separate Simalungun District be established in the HKBP. The Ephorus had repeatedly denied this request. As soon as the HKBP became independent under Ephorus K. Sirait, the request was made once more. Ephorus Sirait himself came to discuss the proposal, and the HKBP Church Board at Pearadja agreed that the Simalungun District would become a separate district in the HKBP with representation on the Church Board.

Under the Japanese all mission schools were taken over by the government and were no longer under the direction of the churches. All church meetings now required the permission of the Japanese government and the churches fell into bad repair. During this time the Komite Na Ra Marpodah, the Kas Saksi Kristus, and the *Madjallah Sinalsal* were discontinued and disbanded. The youth were conscripted into the military, and instead of hymns the children were allowed to sing only songs taught in the schools.

In 1942 seventy Simalungun Christians, led by Djaramin Garingging and his assistant Poltak Saragih, began the movement called Paguruan Saksi ni Kristus (Witnesses For Christ). After ten monthly meetings, in which they studied the Old and New Testament, church history, and the geography of the Holy Land, each student was assigned to two months of practical experience, followed by an examination. The graduates were certified to evangelize without salary throughout Simalungun villages. This project flourished when other church activities were discontinued under the Japanese occupation. The Simalunguns explained to the Japanese military that the PSK was modeled after the work of the famous Japanese theologian Dr. Toyohito Kagawa and thus secured

Japanese support. Soon the project included three hundred registered students from Pematang Raja alone.

The songs of the PSK were heard everywhere and their volunteers spread the gospel throughout Simalungun. The graduates of the PSK formed an organization with a leader, staff, a central office at Pematang Raja, and branches throughout the districts, ressorts, and congregations. By 1963 graduates of the PSK courses numbered 2,038 and it was recognized as an official organization for evangelization throughout Simalungun. Meetings were held once a year at the head office in Pematang Raja, every six months in the districts, every three months in the ressorts, and once a month in every congregation. The group started publishing the newspaper *Pangarah* on an irregular schedule in 1958.

War and revolution had depleted the resources of the church and trained personnel were urgently needed. The ninety-two congregations and 21,600 Simalungun Christians were served by four pendeta. Each pendeta cared for about five thousand church members and was expected to work among non-Christians in his spare time. The Simalunguns responded by opening a class for Bible women at Pematang Raja, with five students, and an institute for training pendeta with seven students in 1950. It was difficult to finance these institutions through the HKBP and a request was sent out through Simalungun congregations that each household contribute rice to support the seven seminary students until they graduated. The students were to receive two years of training at Pematang Raja, a year of study at the HKBP headquarters in Pearadja, followed by at least ten years of practical experience in the Simalungun congregations. It was understood that after graduation the students would be assigned to the Simalungun area.

In spite of difficulties the first class of seven students was finally ready to graduate on Sunday, September 28, 1952. Ephorus Dr. J. Sihombing, several praeses of the HKBP, and other pendeta arrived at Pematang Raja for the graduation ceremonies. However, shortly before the ceremonies a letter arrived from the HKBP headquarters at Pearadja indicating that only three of the pendeta would work in the Simalungun District and the rest would be assigned to other areas in the HKBP. The Simalunguns felt this violated their earlier agreement with the HKBP headquarters.

In this emergency the Simalungun District held a meeting. This first Great Synod of the HKBP Simalungun was led by Praeses Kerpanius Purba and Pendeta A. Wilmar Saragih, inviting members from the Simalungun District to discuss the shortage of ordained pendeta in Simalungun. On October 5, 1952, members of the Synod of the Simalungun District met and referred the problem to the congregations. It was the opinion of the assembly that the HKBP headquarters were opposed to intensive evangelization among the Simalungun. For this reason and due to a shortage of pendeta in the HKBP the four students from Raja had been assigned to other districts in the HKBP, allowing only three students to the Simalungun District. The Special Synod considered that decision unjustified. They demanded that all seven pendeta be assigned to the Simalungun District as had previously been agreed and proceeded to sever relations with the HKBP, withdrawing to form a Great Synod of the HKBP Simalungun. They elected a Chairman, J. Wismar Saragih, and a Secretary General, A. Wilmar Saragih, plus eight others to constitute a Church Board of the HKBP Simalungun. That Church Board assigned the seven pendeta to positions in the Simalungun area and sent a report of these decisions to HKBP headquarters at Pearadja, as well as to the other Indonesian churches and the Indonesian government. Three districts were formed with offices at Pematang Raja, Saribudolok, and Tebing Tinggi, and a central office at Pematang Siantar was established on November 30, 1952.

In their letter to the Ephorus of the HKBP the Simalunguns prefaced their declaration of independence with a paragraph expressing thanks to the HKBP for all the help and assistance they had received in the past and pledging continued recognition of the HKBP Ephorus as supreme church authority for the Simalunguns. They retained the name of the HKBP and ascribed to the same confession and constitution, but their headquarters were now in Pematang Siantar. The Simalunguns declared their independence in working among other Simalunguns, sharing fellowship with other Indonesian Protestant churches, and in contacting foreign missionary organizations for financial aid. The declaration was kept out of the newspapers to prevent public misunderstanding and the prayers of the HKBP were solicited for the new HKBP Simalungun church.[2]

At first the government attempted to bring the disagreement to a harmonious solution without separation, but after further investigation they decided that this was purely a church problem which could only be settled through the separation of the HKBP Simalungun from the HKBP. A four-member committee from Pearadja met with the Board of the HKBP Simalungun to discuss the problem. Actually, the Simalungun District Board had ceased to exist after October 5, 1952; but Pendeta K. Purba and Pendeta A. Wilmar Saragih, who had led that Board, were authorized to meet with the committee by the HKBP Simalungun in spite of this technicality. The Ephorus of the HKBP, Dr. J. Sihombing, visited the head office of the HKBP Simalungun advising that they return to the HKBP as before, promising that nothing would be allowed to interfere with the evangelization of the Simalunguns. However, the split was final.

Missionary H. Volmer from the RMG, who had left Sumatra before the War, now returned to work among the Simalunguns. Although the Simalunguns were glad to receive him back they were disappointed to hear that the Ephorus had ordered him not to begin work among the Simalunguns before the church problem was solved. Missionary Volmer used this time to refine his Simalungun translation of the New Testament and a collection of Bible stories that had been printed by the Dutch Bible Society.

Dr. D. R. Williams, sent to the HKBP by the LWF to direct the Simalungun hospital, was also directed by Pearadja to

2 Letter from the HKBP Simalungun to the Ephorus HKBP, October 15, 1952, CYCOM, National Lutheran Council, Exhibit D, Indonesia, Agenda, September 29, 1953, p. 1.

postpone his work among the Simalunguns for the time being. The HKBP had not yet agreed to the Simalungun request for a hospital to be built by the Lutheran World Federation. Some wanted the hospital located at Raja among Christian Simalunguns. Others felt it should be at Saribudolok, providing closer contact with non-Christians from Serdang, Karo, Dairi, and Samosir. Another problem was whether the hospital would be established by the HKBP or the HKBP Simalungun. Pearadja and the LWF made it clear that the hospital was being given to the HKBP although it would be erected in the area of Simalungun Bataks. The Simalunguns hoped the hospital would help evangelization among other Simalungun Bataks, but the problem for the HKBP was that those brought into the church through the hospital would join the now separate HKBP Simalungun. Finally, Pearadja agreed that the hospital should be turned over to the HKBP Simalungun. It was also decided to locate the hospital near Saribudolok, with the understanding that the congregation there would share financial responsibility for this institution. The Simalunguns established a committee for the Bethesda Hospital to manage its affairs outside the jurisdiction of the HKBP.

A meeting of HKBP and HKBP Simalungun delegations at Pematang Siantar in January, 1953, decided that the HKBP Simalungun should have autonomous status but that some relationship with the HKBP should be retained. The Simalungun church would be able to hire, assign, and fix salaries for its workers, handle its own financial affairs in collecting funds, and work among Simalungun-speaking people whenever and wherever possible. The Simalunguns shared the confession, regulations, and liturgy of the HKBP, recognized the same Great Synod as ultimate authority, and shared the same seminary and government representation.[3] The meeting decided: (1) the seven pendeta would be posted to the

---

3 Proceedings of the Meeting held at Pematang Siantar on the 21st and 22nd of January, 1953, Regarding the Independence of HKBP Simalungun, CYCOM, National Lutheran Council, Exhibit D, Indonesia, Agenda, September 29, 1953, p. 1.

HKBP Simalungun, (2) missionaries Volmer and Dr. Williams would begin work among the Simalunguns, and (3) two members from the HKBP Simalungun would be appointed to the Reconstruction Committee of the HKBP to represent the Simalunguns to foreign mission societies.

The independent Simalungun church was free to call its own Synod, elect its own Church Board, and appoint personnel to positions of leadership, but it was still within the HKBP. This meant that connections with other churches and foreign mission organizations could only be made through the HKBP. In August, 1961, there was a meeting of the Simalungun Church Board to establish a plan for complete separation from the HKBP. The HKBP Simalungun was not impulsive in this move but sought the advice of other churches and organizations. A representative of the Indonesian Council of Churches, while attending the Centennial celebration of the HKBP, met with the Secretary General of the HKBP Simalungun on October 10, 1961. The next day that delegation also met with Dr. Wilm from Westphalia and other representatives of the RMG. On November 24, 1961, they consulted with the LWF representatives G. O. Reitz and Dr. E. Kayser. In December, 1961, there was a meeting with Ephorus Dr. J. Sihombing to discuss complete independence to facilitate evangelization among the Simalungun Bataks. After several meetings it was decided that the Church Boards of the two churches should meet in June, 1962, to determine the future. A committee in the HKBP Simalungun began work on a constitution and other preparations were made for independence. The two Church Boards met on June 15, 1962, at Nommensen University in Pematang Siantar with thirty-one present from the HKBP and eleven from the HKBP Simalungun. The conclusion of the meeting was that the Simalungun church would become completely independent, the details to be worked out by a committee with five representatives from each church as soon as possible and by October, 1963, at the latest.

The HKBP Simalungun immediately applied for membership in the Indonesian Council of Churches, sent a representative to the East Asian Christian Conference meeting in Singapore, and applied for membership in the LWF. Both the LWF and the RMG expressed full satisfaction with the previous arrangement but were willing to support the independent Simalungun church as well if it would facilitate evangelization and be agreeable to the HKBP.

The newly independent Simalungun church adopted the name Geredja Kristen Protestant Simalungun (GKPS) when it was officially established in 1964. The membership totaled 61,147. There were 177 congregations, twenty-two pendeta, three districts, and sixteen ressorts.[4] Their youth group, the Namaposo Kristen Protestant Simalungun (NKPS), formed on December 26, 1953, included fourteen subdivisions and 160 organized groups. The women's work, called Humpulan Parinangon, was organized on March 17, 1961, under the leadership of Bible women and theologically trained seminary graduates such as Minaria Sumbajak. The Bethesda hospital, established in 1953, had begun a course for training nurses under the direction of LWF Missionary Dr. E. Kayser after 1957. There were also medical clinics established in Saribudolok, Haranggaol, Pematang Raja, and Sibuntuon.

The separation of the HKBP from the HKBP Simalungun was described as analogous to the condition *mandjae,* where a son on reaching maturity leaves home and begins exercising independent responsibility as a member of the community. When the son establishes his own household with his own family he achieves independence before his neighbors with a voice in settling internal and external community problems. This is contrasted with political independence *(merdeka),* achieved through revolution and violent disagreement, in having retained a bond of love and concern between the separated parties.

> There is a similarity between the use of mandjae according to Batak Adat and its application to a religious setting in that both parties act in the context of God's love. There is also a difference in that according to Adat it is the parent who

4 Report of the Indonesian Council of Churches (DGI), Djakarta, May, 1964.

initiates the separation while in the establishment of the GKPS it was not the HKBP acting as parent and the HKBP Simalungun as child since the Father of both is God.[5]

Although the two churches remained united in the context of God's love, there was now legal separation of organizations even though both parties retained their common doctrines of belief and confession of faith.

The GKPS has continued to develop. Recently a Religious Training Center was opened at Pematang Raja in buildings financed jointly by the RMG and the LWF. Two German deaconesses are already in Siantar ready to begin work at the Center in the training of Bible women. In addition youth retreats and other courses are also being planned, including a primary school, insuring maximum use of the buildings. There is also an Agricultural Project underway with emphasis on practical training and seed production. This project, which has already begun in Pematang Siantar, is directed by a German and an Indonesian agriculturalist. Finally, the translation of the Old Testament into Simalungun is being printed by the Baden Penerbit Kristen (Christian Publishing Company) for release in 1970. Soon the first complete Bible in the Simalungun language will be published.

The Ephorus of the GKPS reported to the 1968 Synod that, although 339 GKPS members had been excommunicated in 1968, the Simalungun church now contains 221 parishes, 82,589 baptized members, 12,258 families, and 2,320 congregational elders. The activities of the GKPS throughout 1967 are chronicled in the baptism of 7,528 persons, serving of 8,737 communicants, and average Sunday attendance of 7,337 persons.

2. Methodist Work Among the Bataks

The Methodists attempted to begin work among the Bataks in the 1890s. In 1891 Hester Needham, who helped establish

---

[5] Djahutar Damanik, "Mandjae," *Pangarah* (Geredja Kristen Protestant Simalungun), XVI, 10 (1963), 28.

American Methodist Episcopal Mission in Singapore about sending a missionary to the Mandailing Bataks, since the RMG was unable to extend its resources that far. She had heard through Mr. Prudy, the traveling English colporteur, that the Methodists from America had been planning to send a missionary into that part of Sumatra for some time. Finally they sent Miss Needham a letter promising to post a missionary among the Mandailing even if they had to "send all the way to America to get one!"[6] With the exception of the Baptists just to the South of Mandailing and the Java Committee just to the North, the area was unevangelized.

Dr. Benjamin Franklin West, a medical missionary from Singapore, visited Sumatra late in 1892, perhaps to investigate the possibility of missionary work. Leaving from Sibolga, where he contacted the RMG, he rode horseback to the Silindung valley and then walked from Tarutung sixty-seven miles south to Padang Sidempuan before returning to Sibolga. West was impressed with the work of the RMG and the possibilities for other missionary organizations to work there, but nothing was done.[7]

The American Methodist Church began work in Sumatra among the Chinese of Medan in May, 1905, through Soloman Pakianathan's English school. Mr. Pakianathan came from Penang and out of his own salary furnished his own support and half the support of a Chinese preacher, and supplied furnishings for the local church.

Missionary Mark Freeman reported to the Netherlands Indies Mission Conference of the Methodist Church in 1920 that the RMG had allowed the Methodists to work among the Chinese who had moved to Pematang Siantar, although this was within territory allocated to the RMG by the Dutch government. For their part the Methodist Mission pledged not to work among the Bataks, "for whom the Rhenish Mission is

6 Hester Needham, God First: Hester Needham's Work in Sumatra, p. 92.

7 B. F. West, "A Trip to Sumatra's West Coast," The Malaysia Message, II, 4 (January, 1893), 34 and II, 5 (February, 1893), 42-43.

doing a large and very successful work."[8] This promise became more and more difficult to keep as the Toba Bataks began to migrate down from Tapanuli along the coast and requested admission into the Methodist churches. Eventually the Netherlands Indies government assigned to the Methodist Mission a large portion of the Asahan jungle region, inhabited by the largely Pardembanan Bataks and Toba Batak emigrants. Following up an exploration of the area by Lamsana Lumbantobing in 1913, Leonard Oeschsli traveled through the Kisaran and Tandjung Balai area several times around 1921. He estimated that there were between four and five thousand Bataks who had not yet entered Islam although the Muslim *hadjis* were actively converting the radjas and it was urgent that work begin immediately. The deciding factor was Missionary Oeschsli's advance knowledge of planned government improvements in the area, including a proposed dam and project to develop extensive wet-rice terraces along the Asahan River. "All of this is certain to draw the Bataks from the hills which are over-populated."[9]

The first Malay to be ordained in the Methodist Church was a Batak. Lamsana Lumbantobing, one of several Bataks who had attended the training school in Java, had been working in the Malay Christian community.[10] He seemed the ideal choice for the Methodists to begin their work among the Bataks. He was to live in Kisaran, supervise the English-language schools in Kisaran and Tandjung Balai, and preach to the Christian Bataks. For over a year the Christian Bataks had requested a missionary, and when in 1921 the Pardembanan radja Tuan Nagori also invited a missionary to begin work, the request could no longer be refused. Missionary Lumbantobing made frequent trips into the jungle to establish outposts among the Pardembanan, and in 1922 he was joined by Missionary N. T. Gottschall, who was posted at

8 Mark Freeman, "Superintendent's Report," Netherlands Indies Mission Conference, 1920, p. 106.

9 Leonard Oeschsli, "Netherlands Indies Mission Conference Report," 1921, pp. 31-32.

10 Nathalie Toms Means, *Malaysia Mosaic* (Singapore: The Methodist Book Room, 1935), p. 122.

Kisaran. However, when Lamsana Lumbantobing was on a month's leave to visit his old home in Tapanuli, the residents there persuaded him to open an English school, with his two sons as teachers. In a report to the North Sumatra Mission Conference, Leonard Oeschsli indicated "without pronouncing any harsh judgments on him for thus leaving his work, we can only express our disappointment that he should have so quickly succumbed after having begun his work in Asahan with such high expectations."[11] Four years later, in 1927, Lamsana Lumbantobing returned to establish Methodist services for Bataks who had migrated from Asahan to the city of Medan.

In 1928-1929 the Methodist work in Java and Dutch Borneo was closed down by the Dutch government, which assigned the different foreign mission organizations to specific areas in the Netherlands Indies. The missionaries, workers and re-sources of the Methodist Church now focused on South Sumatra and the East Coast Province from 25 miles north of Medan to the Asahan jungles.[12]

With increased migration from Tapanuli the work grew so rapidly that the Superintendent of the mission reported in 1927 that, "on the whole our evangelistic work among the Bataks has shown more signs of encouragement than has our work among the Chinese."[13] Many Bataks, converted to Christianity under the RMG, had moved to the Asahan valley in order to seek employment and land. The RMG did not have enough missionaries to station a man there permanently so an agreement was made with the Methodists to care for Christian Bataks who settled in their area. The Methodists and RMG agreed that should any Batak families return to Tapanuli they would be received back as members of the Batak Church in good standing. Before this agreement there had been some misunderstanding between the Methodists and

11 Leonard Oeschsli, "North Sumatra Mission, Superintendent's Report," 1923, pp. 15-16.

12 G. R. Senior, "Christian Opportunity in Indonesia," 1967, McGilvary & Son, Kirkcaldy, p. 8.

13 R. L. Archer, "North Sumatra Mission, Superintendent's Report," 1927, p. 151.

the RMG. One Batak Christian reported that "the German missionaries, their goeroes and pendetas, had put them on their guard against the Methodists."[14] The policy in 1931 was to accept members in spite of this opposition.

Several possible solutions were proposed to facilitate cooperation between the American Methodist Episcopal Mission and the RMG. A recommendation was made to the General Conference of 1932 that an enabling act be passed "whereby the Batak Christians under the care of the Sumatra Mission Conference may be allowed to form, together with the Batak Christians of the Rhenish Mission, a Batak Protestant Church, at any time during the next quadrennium when this may seem feasible."[15] The object was to allow the Methodist Mission to participate in the spread of Christian culture throughout Sumatra. Another possibility that was seriously discussed was that the small community of Bataks connected with the American Methodist Episcopal Mission merge with the RMG allowing the Methodist Mission to withdraw from the area, as had two of the Dutch missionary societies in South Sumatra, handing over work to the RMG.[16]

There were several projects on which the Methodists and the RMG actively cooperated. The congregation of Tapanuli Christians at Palembang had been without a pendeta for several years while a member of the congregation led the services. At first the Methodist Mission was approached by members and leaders of the congregation asking for spiritual guidance. This was followed by a formal request from the Great Synod of the Batak church to assist their congregation in Palembang. According to this agreement the Methodist pendeta Cleopas Lumbantobing served the Palembang Batak congregation every other Sunday and they, in turn, contributed to his salary.[17]

---

[14] Asahan Circuit, "North Sumatra Mission Report," 1927, pp. 160f.

[15] A. V. Klaus, "Memorials to the General Conference, 1932," General Conference Report, 1931, p. 63.

[16] "Survey of Missions," *International Review of Missions*, XXIII, 89 (January, 1934), 30.

[17] A. H. Prussner, "Palembang District," Sumatra Mission Conference Report, 1937, p. 27.

The Methodist missionary Vera M. Edborg began work among the Batak girls, establishing an organization modeled after the "Camp Fire Girls" organization in America, substituting Batak arts and crafts for those of the American Indian. This organization was united to the church as an agent for training the girls in Christian service. Discussing this plan with Dr. E. Verwiebe, who was then representing the German YMCA organization among Batak youth, a plan was worked out to establish the organization throughout Batakland. One of the RMG missionaries at Laguboti, Miss Viering, organized a group of girls there with thirty members, using the Methodist plan.[18] When Miss Edborg was invited to speak at several congregations throughout the Silindung valley she was approached by others seeking to form similar groups in their congregations. Consequently, attempts were made to hold a semiannual, joint meeting of the Methodist and RMG groups. Miss Edborg was on good terms with the RMG missionaries, having spent three months at Laguboti and three weeks at Pearadja while studying the Batak language.

There were other signs of goodwill besides these projects of cooperation. Missionary Klaus reported to the Sumatra Conference in 1931 that "the missionaries of the Rhenish Mission always encourage the people who move into our territory to unite with us. They would be happy to withdraw their workers from every center where the Methodist Mission is at work."[19] There were, however, problems in working with the Batak Christian migrants. There was a spirit of unrest among the Christian Bataks at Tandjung Balai in 1931, and some of the Batak Christians at Kisaran actually organized an independent church for a period of time although generally the Christian Batak emigrants provided the leadership for the young Methodist churches.[20]

The work among Pardembanan Bataks was done in com-

---

[18] Vera M. Edborg, "Medan District Evangelistic Work," Sumatra Mission Conference Report, 1932, pp. 24-25.

[19] A. V. Klaus, "Report of Mission and District Superintendent," Sumatra Mission Conference Report, 1931, pp. 58-59.

[20] "District Superintendent's Report," Sumatra Mission Conference Report, 1932, pp. 24-25.

petition with Muslims. "The fact that most of the local government officials are Mohammedans gives to Mohammedanism a glamour that Christianity does not yet possess. Every Mohammedan is a brother of the Mohammedan official and is, therefore, in a position to receive favours from him."[21] Islam had preceded the work of missions by only a few years. Many of the Batak communities had gone over to Islam only two or three years before the Methodist missionaries became active in the area. The pressure of Islamizing was particularly strong in communities close to the main arteries of commerce and in large population centers, but evident in rural areas as well. When a new convert to Methodism fell seriously ill in one Batak community and a small boy of the family died, the community's adverse reaction was immediate. " 'Certainly a sign of the disapproval of the ancestral spirits,' said their pagan neighbors. 'Certainly a sign of the wrath of Allah,' said those of their neighbors who had recently become Moslems."[22] But when the Methodists sent trained medical help and the woman recovered, this apparent defeat was turned into a victory. The success of the mission continually hung on the immediate welfare of its most recent converts. The pressure of economic depression was cutting into the Methodist work during the 1930s, but it was decided that the work in Batak villages would be the last to suffer from lack of assistance. "The work among the pagan Bataks is the most encouraging, and the most nearly indigenous work we have. As yet there are no attractions in these villages other than the school and the church."[23]

The work among Bataks in the cities was also increasing, with eighteen congregations of Christian Bataks in the towns along the east coast of Sumatra by 1934.[24] Many of the Batak Methodists from Asahan moved to cities such as Medan and

21 A. V. Klaus, "Superintendent's Report," Sumatra Mission Conference, 1931, pp. 25-26.

22 Fred Chadwick, "Asahan District Woman's Work," Sumatra Mission Conference Report, 1931, pp. 61-62.

23 A. V. Klaus, "Superintendent's Report, 1931," op. cit., p. 26.

24 "District Superintendent's Report," Sumatra Mission Conference Report, 1934, pp. 82-83.

requested to continue their relationship there with the Methodist Church. This posed a difficult problem of comity. "We accept no members who come to us from the congregation of the Rhenish Mission here in Medan. Those who desire to come to us from either of the two independent Batak congregations are received as preparatory members only after we are convinced that their motives in desiring to unite with us are as they should be."[25] Much of the work in the Methodist Medan District, especially around Tebing Tinggi, focused on the Simalungun Bataks. Miss Elsa Schwab, a trained nurse, arrived from Germany in 1932 to work among the Simalungun villages.[26]

The invasion of Holland in May, 1940, caused all the German missionaries to be interned and cut off the Dutch missions from their source of funds. Since several of the Methodists were Swedish and therefore neutrals, they were not interned. Several Americans married to Swedish missionaries also escaped internment. Missionary Ragnar Alm, who had arrived from Sweden in 1931, was appointed to Batak work in the Asahan region after spending a year studying the Batak language and customs. During this time missionary work among the Bataks was carried on by Luther and David Hutabarat. War brought a number of necessary adjustments. Many Methodist Bataks moved back to Tapanuli, or moved out into villages along the coast to begin farming. The work among Methodist youth was discontinued and the two Methodist theological students had to leave Sipoholon seminary when their Dutch and German faculty members were interned. Having completed one-and-a-half years of theological study, these two men, Wismar Panggabean and Stuurman Hutabarat, were transferred to Kisaran where Missionary Alm supervised their studies for an additional half-year.[27]

By 1940 Batak work in the Methodist Church included

25 A. V. Klaus, "Superintendent's Report," Sumatra Mission Conference Report, 1931, pp. 28-29.

26 A. V. Klaus, "The Methodist Church Completes Its First Fifty Years in Sumatra," n.d. (typescript), p. 5.

27 Ragnar Alm, "Deli-Asahan Batak District Report," Sumatra Provisional Annual Conference, 1943, p. 20.

fifty-six congregations served by six pendeta and a group of evangelists. There were twenty schoolteachers and one missionary in an area extending from 195 kilometers north to 200 kilometers south of Kisaran. The work included an estimated four thousand Batak Christians and fourteen schools in which Batak was the language of instruction. Some concern was expressed that the Batak Methodists were grudging in their financial support of the church. While the RMG had pursued a policy of rapid expansion the Methodist Church held that "until we can improve the quality of the Christianity that is lived among us, we had better hesitate to advocate unlimited expansion."[28]

During Dutch Police Action against the Republic of Indonesia from 1945 to 1949, the Bataks fled to the rural countryside and the Chinese fled to the cities. After July, 1947, the Methodist work among the Bataks and Chinese was divided into two groups, each under different political regimes. The group within the Republic territory was led by Ephrim Sihombing and Wismar Panggabean including about twenty preaching points and a number of schools. Although connections were reestablished in February, 1949, communication was still difficult due to political turmoil. Some of the congregations disappeared entirely.[29] The same conditions existed in Tapanuli. When the Methodist pendeta David Hutabarat returned to Tapanuli in 1949 for his first visit in six years, he found the number of people attending Sunday services on the increase, but "spiritually the church is rather low and weak. Recently pamphlets were scattered among the Batak people charging some prominent workers in the church of many things, which, if true, would prove the deplorable state in which the HKBP finds itself now."[30]

There was considerable disharmony in the relations be-

28 A. V. Klaus, "Report of the Batak Work," Sumatra Provisional Annual Conference Report, 1949, p. 18.

29 Luther Hutabarat, "Asahan District Report," Sumatra Provisional Annual Conference Report, 1949, p. 18.

30 David Hutabarat, "Tebing Tinggi, District Report," Sumatra Provisional Conference Report, 1950, p. 32.

tween the Methodist Church and the HKBP during this time. The HKBP was accused of attacking the Methodist work among the Bataks during the 1951 Great Synod, saying that the Batak Methodists were only "hitch-hiking" and that the Methodist Church was only for Chinese. The Methodists were able to justify accepting migrants from the HKBP who would otherwise move into the Catholic, Adventist, or some other church in Sumatra. Wherever the one church would establish a new congregation, the other church would also begin one. The Bataks from Tapanuli maintained that all Christian Bataks were originally from the HKBP and that the HKBP was the only Batak church in Sumatra. There had been an unwritten agreement that members of the HKBP could become members of the Methodist Batak congregations and that the reverse could also occur. But as the migration of Toba Bataks to the Methodist territory along the coast had increased, so had the tension between the two churches. A meeting at Siantar in 1951 between representatives of the Methodist Mission and the HKBP reaffirmed this unwritten agreement, appointed a committee to work toward the union of the two churches, and formulated a declaration to go before the Great Synod of the HKBP for approval. Although the Ephorus referred to the declaration in his annual report, the matter was never referred to committee nor was the Great Synod asked to reaffirm any agreement.[31] The other Indonesian churches were critical of this unnecessary interchurch competition.[32]

The Batak Preachers' Training School of the Methodist Church completed its first year on September 25, 1954, with four students and their families enrolled. Wismar Panggabean was teaching the Old and New Testament, Mrs. Alm taught English, and Mr. Alm taught systematic theology, homiletics, church history, pastoral theology, introduction to the New

---

[31] Fredrik A. Schiotz, Notes Covering a Conference of Dr. Williams and Dr. Schiotz with Dr. Cartwright and Missionary Alm, February 8, 1952, CYCOM, National Lutheran Council, Exhibit, Indonesia, Agenda, February 15, 1952, p. 2.

[32] Th. Müller-Krüger, *Sedjarah Geredja di Indonesia,* p. 203.

Testament, and church discipline. The academic year was divided into four eleven-week quarters with twenty-seven hours of classwork every week.[33] At the beginning of the next academic year, October 4, 1954, two new students entered: Philomen Sirait, who had completed one year at Sipoholon, and a student from the PKB at Palembang. This institution, which came to be called Sekolah Guru Indjil, was located in Kisaran as a training school for Batak teacher-evangelists and Bible women. It was not considered to be a permanent institution but attempted to meet the immediate shortage of theologically trained personnel since no student had been received from Sipoholon for some years. By 1957 there were eight students, all with families, who had finished elementary school and four young women who had all completed the same level of education. One student had been sent there from the HKBP.[34] By 1958 Missionary Alm, the Principal of SGI, had begun teaching at Nommensen University, the new theological training center of the HKBP. After the graduation exercise at SGI in July the plan was to close the school and cooperate with other Sumatra churches at Nommensen. There were nineteen graduates from the Sekolah Guru Indjil that year.[35]

Recognizing the need for trained workers at a pre-university level the Medan Methodist Bible School, started by the Chinese District of the Sumatra Methodist Church in 1954, accepted its first class of non-Chinese students in January, 1964. Two Batak girls and five Batak boys were admitted for a three-year Diploma course. This made the Bible School unique as "the only religious institute in the whole of Indonesia where Chinese and non-Chinese students are preparing for the Christian ministry together, and yet receiving instruction in their own language — the Chinese in Chinese

33 Ragnar Alm, "Report from Batak Preachers Training School," Sumatra Provisional Annual Conference Report, 1955.

34 "The Batak Training School," Sumatra Provisional Annual Conference Report, 1957, p. 162.

35 Ragnar Alm, "Batak Methodist Training School," Sumatra Provisional Annual Conference, 1958, pp. 49-50.

Mandarin, and the non-Chinese in Indonesian."[36] There are a number of Methodist schools in Sumatra, the largest being in Medan with 3,000 students and 100 teachers. In October, 1965, a Methodist University was opened with faculties in Literature and Economics. The university does not receive financial help from the mission boards and is financially dependent on students' fees, drawing staff from the University of North Sumatra and Nommensen University to teach evening courses at the Chinese Methodist school in Medan.

At the Sumatra Annual Conference in January the delegates voted to ask the General Conference of the Methodist Church in America for permission to become autonomous later the same year. In the nationalistic fever of Indonesia's confrontation with Malaysia and Western imperialism a group of extremists lobbied for immediate secession from the Singapore-centered Methodist Church. When this extremist group was voted down they withdrew to form the "Geredja Methodist Merdeka Indonesia" (The Indonesian Free Methodist Church). The pastor of Medan's largest Batak Methodist congregation joined the rebels and continued to occupy his church building. The next Sunday, therefore, there were two congregations and two preachers worshiping at the same time and in the same church. "The two sections glowered at each other and since there are two pulpits in the church the pastors occupied one each. The result, as one can imagine, was chaos — two preachers announcing different hymns and preaching different sermons. It was a blessing when our own pastor, primarily because the 'rebel' had the loudest voice, gracefully retired from the field of battle and let his adversary take what dubious honor can be gained from such an exhibition of Christian disunity."[37] The next Sunday an armed police guard was called in and forcibly removed the Free Methodist pastor from the pulpit. In the midst of revolutionary and nationalistic propaganda surrounding Indonesia's anti-Malaysia campaign, the schism took a political turn with threats and accusations, some appearing in newspaper ad-

36 Senior, *op. cit.*, pp. 10-11.
37 *Ibid.*, p. 18.

vertisements, calling on all Methodists to become "true sons and daughters" of the Indonesian Revolution by joining the Free Methodist Church. Today the Free Methodist Church continues with two congregations in Medan and one at Simpang Dolok and one at Wingfoot to the south, although their small membership includes only one ordained minister.

The Methodist Church of Indonesia now has five districts — four in North Sumatra and one in South Sumatra. In the cities most of the members are Chinese although many congregations use the Indonesian language and include Bataks, Javanese and others in their membership. There are three Batak Districts; one in Rantau Parapat, one in Kisaran and the Medan-Tebing Tinggi District, each working largely among the Simalungun and Toba Bataks. "The Church is governed by a Ketua (Chairman), a Wakil Ketua (Vice-Chairman) and a General Secretary. These three form the Dewan Pimpinan Pusat or Central Governing Body of the autonomous church and in actual fact take the place of the Bishop in the American Methodist Discipline. There are some 35,000 full and preparatory members in the five districts and these are served by 44 ministers and 59 Gospel teachers."[38] The Chairman of the Methodist Church was a Batak, Rev. W. Panggabean, while the Vice Chairman in the first election was a Chinese, "indicating the excellent way in which the Church, which is 80 percent Batak, has integrated the Chinese."[39]

By August, 1964, when the Methodist Church in Sumatra became an independent church, there were thirty thousand members, fifty-two congregations, and eight pastors. The work of Bataks such as Cleopas Lumbantobing, Jethro Manulang, David Hutabarat, and Luther Hutabarat had made a considerable contribution to the work of the Methodist Church among both the Chinese and the Bataks in that church. Ba-

---

38 *Ibid.*, p. 20.

39 Annual Report, 1967, Board of World Missions of the Methodist Church. Presented to the Twenty-eighth Annual Meeting, Denver, Colorado, January 5-15, 1968, p. 88.

taks now made up a considerable part of the Methodist Church.

3. THE KARO CHURCH

The Karo Batak region extends from the north side of Lake Toba up to the Deli area around Medan, with much of that mountainous region sparsely inhabited. The lowlands were adaptable to plantations, which later spread to the highland plateau as well, bringing with them modernizing influences. The plantations of rubber, hemp, tobacco, tea, and other cash crops were constantly harassed by the local Karo Batak inhabitants, who feared that these foreign influences would destroy their traditional way of life. Consequently, tobacco warehouses were burned down, fields of crops destroyed, and the profits of the companies thereby severely diminished. The Karo retreated into the highlands and Dusun region forcing the plantations to import large numbers of Chinese and coastal Malays as laborers.

A director from one of these companies proposed that missionaries be brought in and Christianity introduced to the Karo, so that they might become more civilized and adapt to encroaching Western culture more easily. The result of his proposal was that "since 1890 work has been carried on by the NZG among the Karo Battas, at the initiative of Mr. Cremer, M. P., and under the auspices of the large tobacco concerns on Sumatra's East Coast."[40] The Dutch Mission Society was at first highly reluctant to accept any offer from the companies to pay for missionary work among the Karo. Although the personnel and resources of the NZG were fully committed elsewhere, no such opportunity to reach the Karo was likely to arise again, so finally they accepted.

On April 15, 1890, Missionary H. C. Kruyt arrived at Belawan Deli with his Menadonese assistant Nicholas Pontoh to arrange for the beginning of NZG work. After three trips from Medan to explore the Karo territories, he decided to establish the first mission station at Buluh Awar, on the

---

[40] E. S. De Klerck, *History of the Netherlands East Indies* (Rotterdam: W. L. & J. Brusse, 1938), II, 516.

main path leading to the Karo highlands. At this time all
travelers to the Karo highlands had to travel by foot carrying
their bundles, such as salt for trading, which would weigh
about eighteen kilograms each. Buluh Awar was one of the
rest areas that had developed along this path. There, with
the assistance of the village chief, he rented a house until
the Deli Company could arrange to have one built for him.
While living among the Karo, studying their language,
treating the sick, and speaking out against gambling and drug
addiction, Missionary Kruyt and Pontoh preached a message
that was not readily understood. It was difficult for the local
inhabitants to believe that these men had not come in their
own interest, as the tobacco companies and other Western
interests had, giving rise to much suspicion.[41]

In January, 1891, Missionary Kruyt and Pontoh went back
to Menado to recruit other assistants, bringing Benjamin
Wenas, Hendrik Pesik, Richard Tampenawas, and Johan
Pinontoan with them on their return. The reason for choosing Menadonese evangelists for Batak missionaries remains
an unexplained mystery. The evangelists lived at Buluh Awar,
visited the surrounding villages, and studied the Karo Batak
language. When Missionary Kruyt suddenly left the mission
field in July, 1892, for unexplained reasons, he was replaced
in December by Missionary Wijngaarden, who came to Buluh
Awar from the island of Savu in the Lesser Sundas. There
were difficulties working among the 250 Karo families in
Buluh Awar, such as the persistent rumor that anyone who
learned to read and write would be inducted into the Dutch
army. By 1893 the Menadonese evangelists were ready to
move into more distant villages and begin their work.

On August 20, 1893, the first six local inhabitants were
baptized, encouraging the missionaries to establish other
mission stations and "evangelism houses" built by the villagers
and staffed by the Menadonese evangelists. By 1894 the mis-

---

41 H. Neumann, "Gegevens Over Het Zendingswerk in de Karo-Bataklanden, van 1890 to 1943," Nederlandse Zendingshogeschool, Oegstgeest,
Bibliotheek, Amsterdam, 1966. (Unless otherwise indicated, material on
the Karo church will be drawn from this source.)

sion had four schools besides the one at Buluh Awar with an enrollment of thirty-nine students. The Karo were requesting instruction and baptism in increasing numbers.

Missionary Wijngaarden died in September, 1894, and was replaced by the noted ethnologist, Missionary Joustra, who arrived in November. Joustra settled at Buluh Awar and began learning the Karo language and customs, leading the first communion service in the Buluh Awar community on April 3, 1896. In 1898 Missionary Joustra made a long journey throughout the Karo highlands, accompanied by several evangelists, visiting Karo Batak population centers such as Berastagi, Sukadjulu, and Seberaja. In December he also made contact with the RMG, visiting the west coast of Sumatra. The RMG was to work closely with the NZG among the Karo.

Although several of the evangelists returned to Menado in 1899, more assistance was secured through the RMG, who loaned Missionary Guillaume to the NZG from May 2, 1899, to December 30, 1904. Missionary Guillaume was assigned to work on the Karo plateau. When the villagers continued to request teachers and medical technicians to vaccinate them against smallpox, the RMG supplied evangelists Nahum Tampubolon and Martin L. Siregar to work under the NZG for an unlimited time. There were many evangelists from the RMG and later the HKBP who worked among the Karo Bataks under the NZG.

The first Karo church building was erected on December 24, 1899, and all the hymns sung at the dedication were in the Karo Batak language. By this time the community at Buluh Awar, with its new church, included sixty-six members, seventeen of whom were baptized and four confirmed, with ninety-three students attending the four mission schools.

There was a great drought and crop failure in 1901 that made the work of missionaries even more difficult. There was much disease spreading among the Karo Bataks, and they had little enthusiasm for new ideas. Several of the evangelists died, and others were forced to return to Menado for health reasons. The missionaries had been attempting to

establish wet-rice terraces in the Karo highlands but the
people were not ready to accept this revolutionary idea any
more than they were willing to accept medical care. However,
the work of education continued, with hand-copied editions
of arithmetic books and *104 Stories of the Old and New
Testament* being distributed in the Karo language. Two new
schools and a medical clinic were constructed with funds
Missionary Neumann, who arrived in April, 1900, supplied
from sources in France and the Netherlands.

The mission received permission to work on the plateau
region in 1902 when the Karo radja Pa Pelita permitted them
to build a mission station at Kabandjahe. Missionary Guillaume sent the materials and a carpenter to begin construc-
tion, but rebellion broke out and all the building materials
were stolen. The missionaries were not discouraged, however,
and Missionary Joustra launched a campaign to establish
wet-rice terraces subsidized by the Deli Company, introducing fruit trees, vegetables, and flowers along with improved
cultivation methods for food crops. This work was assisted
by the Dutch-appointed Controleur for Batak affairs, C. J.
Westenberg, who did much for the Karo Bataks and strongly supported the work of the mission.

An epidemic of animal diseases swept through the Karo
country in 1904, so severe that in the Sibolangit community
only eight pigs survived. This was an extreme hardship for
the primarily agricultural economy. Increasingly the people
realized the necessity of medical assistance, accepting three
additional medical technician–evangelists from the RMG.
Additional schools were being established and the mission
opened a trading store on the plateau highlands, both as a
service to the local Karo people and as a local source of funds.

In 1905 Missionary Joustra left the mission field to return
to Holland. While this was a serious loss, Joustra was able
to help the Karo Bataks through numerous programs for
research, translation of materials, and technical assistance
when he became Archivist of the Leiden Batak Institute in
1908.

Civilization was spreading rapidly throughout Karoland.

"Writing in 1916 Lekkerkerker states that when the Dutch came to Karoland they abolished slavery, fixed a maximum bride price, registered the population, collected all firearms, made the village heads into part of the state apparatus and paid them, first controlled then ended the opium trade, vaccinated the people, and made other sanitary regulations, prohibited abortion, levied taxes, set up markets and regulated them, and erected a few schools."[42] The government had completed a road down the mountains from the highlands to Medan. The educational work expanded accordingly, with two new schools and an evangelism staff of eighteen men serving fourteen Karo communities. Everyone wanted to attend school, causing a serious shortage of facilities and teachers. Missionary G. Smit opened a teacher-training school at Berastagi which was later moved to Raja in 1909. The school consisted of one newly constructed schoolhouse and two temporary shelters for dormitories. By 1909 the number of teachers had grown to twenty-eight and the mission was securing government subsidy for nine of its schools.

The mission was especially active publishing literature in the Karo language. An almanac had been published periodically and other books used in the schools were continually being released. An official, government-recognized legal oath in Karo Batak was designed for the Karo law courts and juridical matters. A translation of Matthew by Missionary Neumann was published in Amsterdam, and the first hymnal for church and school was published in 1916. Missionary Neumann translated the book of Acts and Joustra revised the translation of *104 Bible Stories*. Missionary Kielstra directed a publication on adat regulations for Christians that resulted in the book *Surat ni adat Kalak Keristan Batak* (An Adat Book for Christian Bataks).

In spite of the rapid growth the mission was in financial

---

42 C. Lekkerkerker, *Land en Volk van Sumatra* (Leiden: E. J. Brill, 1916), quoted in D. H. Penny and Masri Singarimbun, "Economic Activity Among the Karo Batak of Indonesia: A Case Study in Economic Change," pp. 31-66 of the *Bulletin of Indonesian Economic Studies*, No. 6, February, 1967, Department of Economics Research, School of Pacific Studies, Australian National University, Canberra, p. 50.

difficulty. The Karo Bataks now had to pay for their medical treatments and there was a fresh attempt to raise money for a hospital at Sibolangit. The mission felt that if the local economy could be helped to prosper this would also help the mission. Consequently, the Batak Institute sent Mr. Botje to Karoland to introduce modern agricultural methods, assisted by three government-appointed advisors in 1910. Mr. Botje settled in Berastagi and later moved to Kuta Gadung, introducing potato and cabbage crops as well as husbandry of Dutch cattle. The agricultural work was transferred to Sungei Sikambing in 1920 when Mr. Botje left Karoland. The Dutch opened a branch of the Bogor Horticultural Gardens at Sibolangit in recognition of the agricultural potential of the Karo highlands. The Batak Institute also established a Batak Vocational School at Kabandjahe about this time.

Missionary van den Berg and the Dutch government officer C. J. Westenberg worked with the local radjas to establish a leprosarium in Karoland. The institution Lau Si Momo (Bubbling Water) was established on August 25, 1906, admitting sixty-nine persons to the mud huts and back rooms of van den Berg's own house, which served as dormitories. The institution grew with the addition of another small dormitory and dispensary to serve the 116 patients in the first year of its existence. By 1912 another leprosarium was built by the government at Kabandjahe to isolate groups of patients for special treatment requiring strict supervision and intensive care not possible in the crowded conditions of Lau Si Momo.

Conditions at Lau Si Momo were further improved in 1918 when Missionary H. G. van Eelen came to work as director. He was to stay for twelve years. Missionary van Eelen did much to improve social conditions for the patients, removing the barbed wire surrounding the institution and electing leaders from among the patients to govern the colony. The new radja of Lau Si Momo immediately placed a sign over his doorway proclaiming, "We are all in good health!" Before Lau Si Momo was established the lepers had simply been cast out of their villages and forced to live in small bamboo huts built by their relatives, who would occasionally bring them food. Sometimes the neglect of these lepers became so intolerable that they would all join together in a hunger riot and invade the countryside.

When Louis Couperus visited the 340 patients at Lau Si Momo, 240 of whom were baptized, he was impressed with how well they were treated, compared with other leper colonies. If they still had hands and feet, and the radja agreed, the patients were allowed to marry. Each patient had a portion of ground and shared his resources with his neighbors. Sometimes when patients were ready for discharge they begged to stay in the colony. There was a shop where goods could be bought and sold and a small church had been built. Among the eighty families there were only four children. The colony had its own elected chief and the adult youth had special quarters for themselves, as in any other Karo village. There was a line drawn in the ground defining the perimeter of the camp, beyond which the patients were not allowed to go. All rubbish was collected and burned in deep holes, making this village considerably cleaner than the ordinary Karo village. On Saturdays every patient would change clothes, putting on freshly washed and disinfected clothing. Mr. Couperus was deeply moved by the scene.

> We pass through their compound. They accompany us with their drum — they were all clad in the dark indigo-blue of the Battas — and they always take care to stand to the windward of us, so that the breeze may not carry any germ toward us. Whenever a wind gets up they quickly crowd to the other side. Miserable creatures! They follow us about with their eyes, especially Mr. van Eelen, who knows them each by name. They work. They have their little field. They do the necessary smith's work. They want to remain here always, they say, for they have no very pleasant recollection of their village, when they were cast out the healthy ones often going after them with choppers. They display the wounds caused by the wrath of their relatives. Here they would like to live and die. If their hands fall off, then they will have the implements bound to their stumps. Over there I see a man creeping along the ground; his feet have gradually fallen off; he is still making

bird cages and wooden shelves. They are human beings, human bodies, and round about their black misery is the sunshine, the golden green paradise of Eden.[43]

The facilities at Lau Si Momo were expanded to include operating rooms and a laboratory. In 1934 Missionary Jansen Schoonhoven went to Lau Si Momo and remained there until the war, caring for the approximately four hundred patients and organizing activities such as a band and sports. Other medical work was also expanding. In 1929 Sister J. M. Meijr came to work at Sibolangit and Kabandjahe, training student nurses there. On June 28, 1933, the hospital at Kabandjahe, which had been sponsored by the Batak Institute, was transferred to the NZG. Some of the doctors there, who had been supplied by the Public Health Service, stayed on, but additional medical staff were urgently needed. Dr. A. E. van Kempen, the first medical missionary to the Karo, came to Kabandjahe and remained there until 1936, assisted by Sister H. Hu Hövers. The hospital facilities at Kabandjahe were expanded to include a women's ward, a children's ward, and a private ward.

One of the most critical problems by 1937 was the shortage of doctors. Dr. Lim Toan Him from West Java arrived to work from 1937 until May, 1938, but most of the doctors were secured from abroad. The hospital at Kabandjahe was being steadily improved with the addition of another main building. Sister Meijr came to Sibolangit and Kabandjahe especially for work in the children's ward, but she died on August 31, 1942. Dr. Lindeboom came for several months along with Dr. Scholten, but the latter died of pneumonia several months later. Although the hospital at Sibolangit finally had sufficient facilities it no longer had a doctor in residence. Finally Dr. Tan Oen Siang arrived from Batavia and remained at the hospital until 1941.

Education remained a primary focus of the mission, although during the 1920s interest among the Karo in education was dwindling rapidly with a reported truancy rate of 80 percent or more in most areas. The mission was forced to

---

[43] Louis Couperus, *Eastward* (London: Hurst & Blackett, 1924), p. 95.

turn most of its schools back to the government and close down others. The Karo apparently lost interest in education after 1919. Eventually the teacher-training college itself closed down, although it was reopened a few years later as an evangelist training center. Experimenting with different educational approaches, a boarding school was established at Kabandjahe accommodating village youth who had moved to the city to attend school. Also a girls' boarding school was set up with Mrs. L. Wilkens from New Zealand acting as housemother until 1935. This effort developed into a Christian advanced elementary school (HIS) at Kabandjahe. Many of the younger generation were going to Medan for secondary school, prompting the establishment of a Christian boarding school in 1932 at Djalan Pertjut under the direction of Pa Pulung. A few years later Mrs. G. Neumann-Bos established the Christelijke Meisjes Club Madju (Christian Girls' Club) aimed at educating young women not only in the Bible but also in home economics, nutrition, sewing, and other practical skills.

Evangelism was not neglected for the sake of these institutions. By 1926 there had been 1,500 baptisms. Several new congregations had been established, and by 1934 there were 4,189 Christians among the Karo. The demand for evangelists had increased to the point that, in January, 1935, an evangelist school was opened at Raja with Missionary Muylwijk as supervisor. As an important factor in evangelism, literature was continuously placed in circulation. Missionary Neumann translated the Letter of Paul to the Romans into Karo, and by 1928 the whole New Testament had been translated into Karo Batak. Missionary Neumann was also active in publishing other books such as *Een Jaar Onder De Karo-Bataks* (A Year Among the Karo Bataks) in 1919, an outline grammar of Karo Batak entitled *Schets Karo-Bataksche Spraakkunst,* and a Dutch translation of the Karo book *Pustaka Ginting* in 1928. Missionary Neumann became known as an authority on the Karo Bataks, and on March 3, 1925, he was appointed Conservator of a museum at Raja to be set up by the Sumatra Committee.

On July 23, 1941, the Karo church held a Synod at Sibo-langit and made two important decisions. First, the system of church regulations was officially accepted, and second, the liturgy was established. Most of the missionaries were present, as were the Batak evangelists, Palem K. K. Sitepu and Thomas L. Sibero. When the Japanese interned all Dutch missionaries the Karo church held another Synod on September 29, 1943, and the Geredja Batak Karo Protestant (GBKP) became an independent church.

There were few immediate changes caused by the coming of the Japanese and the ministers were generally allowed to continue their work. But this tolerance did not last long. At the advice of Dr. Kleijn the elderly prisoners were allowed to be interned at the hospital at Kabandjahe, while the non-missionary personnel were interned in the boarding school complex of the Planters Schools Vereeniging at Berastagi. The leprosarium at Lau Si Momo needed nursing personnel, so the elderly were put to work there until the end of 1943, when nearly everyone was forcibly interned. Berastagi was se-lected as the initial internment camp but the inmates were transferred later to the notorious camp of Aik Pemingge for women and Si Renggo-renggo for men. At Aik Pemingge, Missionary J. van Muylwijk died on January 22, 1945, of malnutrition and disease.

Of the medical staff, Dr. Bremmer, Dr. Kleijn, and Dr. Smal-braak were allowed to continue working under the Japanese. Dr. Kleijn traveled by bicycle to visit the far-flung medical clinics and to search for medical supplies in Medan. When these doctors were finally interned and transported to Singa-pore, their ship was torpedoed and they all died in 1944. Since it was in the best interests of the Japanese, Dr. Smal-braak was allowed to continue working under strict super-vision and was even allowed to continue using his car to visit medical clinics at Pantjur-Batu, Penen, and Biru-biru, but finally he also was interned on May 6, 1945.

After the war all the missionaries except Missionary Neu-mann and his wife returned to Holland. Missionary Neumann remained in Medan and continued to serve the Karo church, leading worship services until the day of his death, November 16, 1949, in Medan. His wife left a few months later for the Netherlands, being then quite ill, to see her children, whom she had not seen for many years. She died June 4, 1950, at Voorburg.[44]

4. ROMAN CATHOLICS

Before the arrival of the first Catholic missionary, Rev. Fr. de Hesselle, in 1854, the Catholics living in North Sumatra who were Europeans, Chinese, and Indians, were served by missionaries from the Vicariat Apostolic of Batavia who annually visited Sumatra.[45] Fr. de Hesselle became ill and was sent to the island of Nias for medical treatment, but died shortly thereafter. While the Dutch had given exclusive permission to the RMG for work among the Bataks, many Bataks had come in contact with Roman Catholicism through visiting the neighboring island of Penang. From 1878 to 1884 Pastoor Wenneker of the Society of Jesus worked in Medan, North Sumatra, to serve the Catholics living there, although he was prohibited from working among the Bataks.

In 1911 the island of Sumatra was separated from the Vicariat Apostolic of Batavia and became an independent mission, entrusted to the Dutch Capuchins under Mgr. Cluts, the first Vicar Apostolic of Sumatra. The Capuchins concentrated on existing Catholics and were refused permission to work among the indigenous populations. The headquarters were established in Padang, far south of the Batak-inhabited region, but requests continued to arrive for missionaries from Batak villages in Tapanuli. Appeals and demonstrations to remove comity restrictions had little effect. The government felt the peace would be jeopardized by competing missionary organizations and the Ecclesiastical Superior had no personnel to send.

Mgr. Cluts died in 1921 and was succeeded by Mgr. Brans,

44 See Chapter V, part 6, for postwar history of the Karo church.

45 Fr. Guido Tharappel, "Catholic Church in Batakland" (Parapat: Seminari Agung [unpublished typescript], 1967). (Unless otherwise indicated, material on the Catholic Church will be drawn from this source.)

who continued to apply pressure on both the government and the church for removal of comity restrictions. Finally, in 1934 formal permission was given to the Capuchins to open their own mission in Sumatra. In exchange the Roman Catholics allowed Protestants to work in South New Guinea, which had been exclusively allocated to the Catholic Mission.[46] The Capuchins opened their first Batak mission work from 1928 to 1932 in Sibolga and Pematang Siantar, followed by work in Balige by 1934. A year after the Catholics began their missionary activity in Batakland there were twenty-three stations in Tapanuli. By the following year there were five main mission stations with resident priests and seventy-seven outstations visited monthly by neighboring missionaries. The Catholic Mission now served approximately 6,000 converts. Schools were established in practically all mission stations staffed by Dutch missionaries. By 1941 there were 27,-943 Catholics, 32,307 catechumens, 22 main churches, and 248 outstations with 208 schools of various grades distributed throughout Batakland.

With the Japanese occupation all Catholic missionaries were placed in concentration camps and the work was left to a few catechists, themselves not well trained in their faith. Bitterness against the Dutch during the Revolution following the war prevented Catholic missionaries, who were almost all Dutch, from returning to work in Batakland. It was only in 1947 that a few missionaries were allowed to return to work among the Bataks. Even then their activities were somewhat restricted. Two or three Javanese priests visited the Sumatran Catholics, but because they were strangers to the Batak language and customs they were unable to provide much help. By 1950 most of the old missionaries and many new ones were active again.

When Padang was made a separate ecclesiastical unit in 1952 under the Italian missionaries of the Congregation of St. Francis Xavier, the Capuchins were able to devote all their attention to the Bataks. By 1953 there were 52,083 Catholics in Batakland, including about 3,000 Chinese and

46 De Klerck, op. cit., p. 525.

non-Bataks, with about 21,000 catechumens. Although many of the mission schools were destroyed or taken over by the government during the Revolution, the work progressed and in 1959 German Capuchin missionaries expelled from China were able to intensify their work in Nias, Sibolga, and the west coast of Sumatra. A minor seminary established in Padang in 1954 was transferred to Pematang Siantar in 1955. This school provided high school education in preparation for ecclesiastical studies toward the priesthood. It now includes about two hundred students with a staff of Dutch, Swiss, and Indian priests and Batak lay-teachers. In 1958 a major seminary was established at Parapat to train candidates for the priesthood. The first Batak Catholic priest was ordained in 1964, studied several years in Rome, and is now working in Medan. Of the thirty-two students at the Parapat Seminary, twenty-one are Bataks. Out of the 260 sisters, belonging to six different congregations, 170 are Bataks. Many Bataks are also being recruited into congregations of brothers as well. Batak Catholic lay workers are spread throughout Indonesia, generally in vocations of nursing or teaching. By 1961 the Vicariat Apostolic of Medan under the Dutch Capuchins was given status as an Archdiocese and Metropolitan See with four suffragan Dioceses. Mgr. Van Den Hurk, the present head of the mission, assumed office as Bishop of the mission in 1955.

Besides the Church, the Catholics are active through a branch of the Catholic Party of Indonesia, the Catholic University Students' Association, the Farmers' Association, and other groups. At present there are seventy-one priests working among the Bataks and three hundred missionary brothers and sisters engaged in educational or charitable activities. There are five Catholic high schools, three teacher-training schools, twenty middle schools, one nursing school, one technical school, one school for the blind, and one for the deaf and dumb. There is a 370-bed modern hospital and another thirty-bed smaller hospital besides fifteen dispensaries where medications are available. In the Archdiocese of Medan there are nearly 143,000 Batak Catholics and in the Prefecture of

Sibolga over 15,000 Batak Catholics. About 6,000 adult Bataks
enter the Catholic Church annually. At present the Bataks
living in Samosir have been particularly attracted to Roman
Catholicism.

> From the results that are seen externally it can be said with-
> out any exaggeration that at present the Batakland is the
> most flourishing Catholic Mission in the whole of Asia. It
> is hoped that with the emergence of native Clergy and re-
> ligious Brothers and Sisters the Catholic Church will become
> still more vigorous and the Bataks will become in course of
> time heralds of salvation to millions of Indonesians who still
> do not know and love Christ, the light of the world.[47]

There has been some bitterness between Protestants and
Catholics in Batakland. Batak Protestants contended that
many new converts to Catholicism had been drawn from
Protestant churches, arguing that well-staffed Catholic mission stations at Sibolga, Siantar, and Medan were unfairly
attracting the young Batak people by offering them good
and well-equipped schools.[48] The HKBP specifically rejects
Catholic tendencies such as Mariolatry, the conception of the
mass as a repetition of Christ's sacrifice mediated through the
priest, the doctrine that the pope in Rome is the vice-regent
of Christ on earth, the efficacy of good works, Purgatory,
masses for the dead, veneration of the saints, and relics.[49]
Numerous brochures and papers have been published by
Batak Protestant churches directed against the Roman Catholics.

The Roman Catholics have made their own contribution
to mutually antagonistic relations. One example is the statement by Mgr. Fulton Sheen in *Worldmission* where he describes the Bataks as one people where the Catholic Church
did not have to work hard to secure many converts. He
considers it "unfortunate that the Roman Catholic Church

---

[47] Tharappel, *op. cit.*, p. 5.

[48] Andar Lumbantobing, "The Confession of the Batak Church," in
Vilmos Vajta and Hans Weissgerber, *The Church and the Confessions*,
pp. 127-28.

[49] *Ibid.*

could not have come in earlier, for the inadequacies of the Rhenish Mission's program meant that the people were not sufficiently prepared to participate in the development of the Indonesian Republic."[50]

In recent years the threat of Communism and the potential threat of radical Muslim groups have drawn Protestants and Catholics closer together. This has been especially true among Christian youth and students. Around the time of the 450th anniversary of the Reformation Rev. Fr. Linus Fäh, O.F.M., Cap, was invited to lecture at Nommensen Seminary, and shortly thereafter Ds. F. Siregar, Dean of the Nommensen Faculty of Theology, was invited to speak at the Roman Catholic Seminary. Both formal and informal contacts have tended to increase. Hopefully these tentative attempts at cooperation can grow into an association to the mutual advantage of all Batak churches.

5. THE PENTECOSTALS AND ADVENTISTS

The first of the Pentecostals to arrive in North Sumatra came as chaplains on American ships and preached in the port towns. Eventually they began receiving invitations to preach at Pematang Siantar and later in Balige among the Bataks around Lake Toba. The Dutch discouraged this activity, begun in the 1920s, considering the Batak area closed to additional missionary organizations. But when Radja Purba of Kabandjahe was converted through studying the Bible and correspondence courses he came to the Pentecostal missionaries for tutoring. Since he returned to work among the people of Kabandjahe and the surrounding area, the Pentekosta Rohulkudus (Holy Spirit Pentecostal) has grown out of his work. This is the largest group of Pentecostals in Batakland, concentrating mostly on the Toba and Karo Bataks.[51]

As the Pentecostals gained support among the Bataks and

---

50 Winburn Thomas, "Indigenous Batak Church Hopeful," *The Christian Century,* October 26, 1955, p. 1254.

51 Howard Gering, "The Pentecostal Church Among the Bataks," 1967 (typescript).

the Dutch government became less sympathetic toward German interests, the comity arrangements were reconsidered. When the Head of the Pentecostal Church from Surabaja approached the Dutch Governor General in 1935 for permission to answer calls of members living in Balige, Tarutung, and throughout Tapanuli, permission was granted. Pendeta P. Simandjuntak, a Batak Pentecostal, was appointed to the work. Later evangelists such as G. N. Pane, son of a Batak Protestant pendeta in Sipirok, joined with Pendeta Simandjuntak, Radja Purba, and Karl Sianturi. Both Pendeta Purba and Simandjuntak had attended the Pentecostal Bible Institute in Surabaja under the care of Missionary W. W. Patterson.

At the institute the students were taught the order of worship for church services, a strong responsibility to evangelize the heathen, and Pentecostal doctrine. The doctrine included: the Deity and Atonement of Jesus Christ; holiness as a doctrine of the Church; premillennialism; the literal return of the Lord Jesus; baptism by immersion in the name of the Trinity; the baptism of the Holy Spirit. Support for the pendeta came either through their own labor or through the tithes and offerings from the local church. The parent church of Geredja Pentakosta di Indonesia is Bethel Pentecostal Temple, Seattle, Washington.

The work advanced most rapidly in villages where no other churches had been established, especially among the Pak-Paks of northwestern Batakland, leading up into Atjeh on the west coast. Rapid growth was also realized in the more settled areas of Balige, Humbang, Samosir, and Sipirok. Churches were also established around Medan on the east coast, although the Muslim Sultans were very unsympathetic toward the churches there. In the poverty-stricken Sidikalang area the pendeta could not be supported by their local congregations, and often a lay-preacher would take on pastoral responsibilities in addition to working his own fields. The local church was expected to assume all costs without foreign support for operation of schools, Bible training institutes, church buildings, evangelization, correspondence courses, publishing, and printing. According to Pentecostal missionary Howard Gering, the four Pentecostal churches working among the Bataks (Geredja Pentakosta di Indonesia, Geredja Pentakosta Indonesia, Geredja Bethel Indjil Sepenuh, and Geredja Pentakosta) have accumulated a large estimated membership.

> Though not recognized by some churches except as a sect, it numbers almost 285,000 members in North Sumatra, divided among four major groups, with over 500 ordained pastors and assistant licensed pastors and 650 other workers. Also included in this number are the independents and smaller congregations not in general fellowship with the major groups. This does not include infants or people born into the church, as the doctrine of the church teaches that to be baptized one must be of age to acknowledge.[52]

Government statistics from 1961 indicate seven different Pentecostal groups that are organizationally separate working among the Bataks. The established Batak churches take a hostile view toward the Pentecostals, holding that "members of these Pentecostal groups are mostly former members of the HKBP, i.e., members under church discipline or who refused to pay their dues to the church."[53]

One sign of Pentecostal advancement is the Bible school erected in Pematang Siantar in 1958. This school, headed by Missionary Howard M. Gering, is supported and was built by the Geredja Pentakosta di Indonesia and is presently under the direction of Pendeta Karl Sianturi. There are fourteen correspondence courses offered and the Pentecostals have been active in publishing books on doctrine, church dogma, reference books, and assorted tracts and nonsectarian leaflets. There is presently an attempt to unite the Pentecostal work in North Sumatra, with plans to educate the ministry for those churches in the Bible school at Pematang Siantar.

Dr. Ralph Waldo Munson began the Seventh-day Adventist work in Sumatra, arriving at Padang on New Year's Day, 1900. Although the group at first worked mainly among the

---

52 *Ibid.*

53 Andar Lumbantobing, "The Confession of the Batak Church," *op. cit.,* p. 132.

Chinese, the first Indonesian to join was Immanuel Siregar, son of the first Batak convert by the RMG at Sipirok.[54] Siregar had come to Padang in 1904 to establish a newspaper. Leaving Padang, Siregar went back to Tapanuli, where he carried on missionary work for the Seventh-day Adventists. He established a school at Balige in 1913, and the next year obtained permission to invite an American family as foreign teachers. But when Missionary and Mrs. B. Judge went to Balige from Padang in 1914 they "found the time 'inopportune,' that is, they were apparently discouraged by the Dutch."[55]

Two Adventists, Missionary W. P. Barto and Missionary Dallas S. Kime, opened a school in Medan during 1916 at 15 Julianastraat (now Djalan Asia). Kime was admitted to Tapanuli in 1922 and established a mission at Sipogu, twelve miles north of Sipirok; but when warned by the Dutch that missions would be forbidden, he changed the mission station into a school. He asked the local radjas to send their most promising youth and 175 students enrolled for his first class. By 1961 the Seventh-day Adventists had an estimated 30,970 members, largely concentrated in the Batak area.[56] The work by Siregar spread to include thirty-nine congregations by the outbreak of the Second World War. The headquarters were moved from Sipirok to Padang Sidempuan in 1934, and to Siantar in 1936. There was a Dutch missionary stationed with the Adventists before the War and several Americans have recently been sent as advisors, but most of the work is carried on by Indonesians. In North Sumatra, S. R. Sitompul and Karel Tambunan, both Bataks, were in charge of Adventist work.

The Adventists are characterized among other Batak churches by "a stern legalism, especially with regard to the Sabbath, tithing, and prohibitions or taboos with regard to

54 James W. Gould, *Americans in Sumatra*, pp. 119-20.
55 *Ibid.*
56 *Ibid.*

foods."[57] The group has an active program of literature distribution, including the magazine *Rumah Tangga* (Home) and other religious literature that the Adventist members sell from door to door. In 1949 they established a training school at Pematang Siantar and they supported a dental clinic in Medan.

6. HURIA KRISTEN INDONESIA

One of the consequences of rapid growth in the Batak Christian community was dissension, division, and jealousy among groups of early converts, who pursued their own understanding of this new religion. This dissension was not only among the early converts but also between nationals and the foreign missionaries. One group of nationals actively agitated for increased independence from foreign control. While many Bataks had chosen to follow the new Christian religion, they had not abandoned their own adat, traditional art forms, and pride in their Batak heritage. Some of these early Batak converts were suspicious that the foreign missionaries were conspiring with the Dutch government to subvert established traditions and pacify the spirit of Batak regionalism.

In 1905 the students of Sekolah Radja Narumonda, an institution of the RMG-Batak church, called a strike. M. H. Manullang, who is now a HKI pastor in Medan, led the 120 students who opposed the school administration. The students, all from Batak Christian families, claimed that German missionaries were exerting pressure to shape the curriculum toward a teaching vocation in congregations rather than the civil service vocation desired by many of the students. The students felt this inhibited their freedom and prevented them from taking advantage of civil service job opportunities. When, as a consequence, the school was closed, most of the students went into business or took up vocational employment according to their training. Three of the students, M. H. Manullang, Immanuel Siregar, and Gajus Sihite, con-

[57] Andar Lumbantobing, "The Confession of the Batak Church," *op. cit.*, p. 132.

tinued to agitate against foreign influences. These three established a newspaper in 1906 called "Binsar Sinondang Batak," roughly translated to mean "A Light Shines in Batakland," which focused on problems in Batak society.

The newspaper actively opposed foreign influences from German missionaries and the Dutch government, accusing missionaries of accumulating profits from their Tapanuli contacts and exploiting the Batak people for the sake of Dutch government subsidies to mission institutions. The RMG was accused of securing trading advantages for Hamburg business interests in return for financial support. All foreigners were accused of violating traditions of Batak society. The paper also actively campaigned to keep foreign plantations from entering Tapanuli, threatening that this would result in loss of land rights, exploitation by middlemen, and further violation of the adat. As a result of these articles persons associated with the newspaper were frequently called before Dutch courts and sometimes put into jail. In 1907 M. H. Manullang, Immanuel Siregar, and Gajus Sihite left for Singapore to study religion and political organization, intending to return and liberate their people.

When M. H. Manullang returned to Batakland he established the "Hatopan Kristen Batak" (Batak Christian Federation) in 1917, aimed at achieving economic and social independence within the framework of Christian ideals. Feeling ran high among the Bataks, and there were reports of churches being opened by force when missionaries refused to allow HKB members to meet there.[58] Branches were set up throughout Batakland emphasizing economic development and opposition to foreign influences. The group worked for unification and progress of the Bataks through political, social, and economic advancement. It affiliated with early nationalist parties such as Insulinde and entered into several business enterprises. "It succeeded in establishing a number of commercial banks, a printing press and a newspaper,

---

58 Crommelin, "The Growth of the Native Church in the East Indian Archipelago and the Development of Christian Character," *International Review of Missions*, XXIII (July, 1934), 372.

and its members ultimately ventured even into estate tobacco production on Sumatra's East Coast in competition with Europeans."[59]

The RMG attitude was interpreted as possessive paternalism that claimed monopolistic control of Batak churches as its right, jealously guarding Batakland against the encroachments of other churches such as the Methodists, Adventists, or Roman Catholics. The group of dissidents among the Batak Christians formulated a resolution stating: (1) that religious matters be clearly separated from civil government influences, (2) that national workers be included in the decision-making bodies of the Batak church, (3) that the churches be democratized, eliminating the authoritarian control of the pendetas, and (4) that a Church Board and Financial Board be established. When action on this resolution was continually postponed and no compromise could be reached, the dissidents organized their own churches.

On May 1, 1927, the Huria Christen Batak (HChB), Mission Batak, Party 123, TOBA (Tabahen Oeng Bahen Arta), which was to gather money for social service projects, and the Perhimpunan Kristen Batak (PKB) all withdrew from the RMG-supported Batak church, excluding foreigners from positions of authority in all spiritual and congregational affairs. Although the dissidents referred to themselves as the "Geredja Zelfstanding" (Self-Standing Church) they were never organizationally united. Party 123 was strong in the Silindung, Humbang, Pahae area, while the TOBA were from the area of Lake Toba, traditionally opposed to Silindung area domination. Party 123 was formed during the early years of the first Medan congregation. This group in Medan had been served for a long time by a Batak pendeta, but as the church grew he was replaced by a German missionary. A petition calling for the reinstatement of this much-loved Batak pastor was signed by 123 persons. Because the TOBA was from a different area it sided with the RMG against Party 123. Although Party 123 was soon dissolved, the dis-

---

satisfaction lingered among members, who turned to the HChB and the Mission Batak.

The largest of the dissident groups was the HChB, established under the leadership of Sutan Malu Panggabean with seventy-five congregations and fifteen thousand members. The HChB set up its own training school at Oeloed, with a foreigner from Surinam as Principal. This school of "domestic economy" with its 130 pupils required an entrance fee of ten guilders and a quarterly school fee to be paid in advance.[60]

The HKBP, established as an independent organization in the 1930 regulations, attempted to appease the dissidents by incorporating many of their suggestions into the new regulations, but the bitterness surrounding the schism was too great. Marriages performed under the RMG-Batak church before the schism were not always recognized by the new churches so that couples divided by the schism sometimes remarried without first securing a divorce. This led to accusations of polygamy from the HKBP. The Dutch government, remembering the 1926 Communist uprising in Padang, suspected the groups to be Communist sympathizers. During the early years members under HKBP church discipline were inclined to join the HChB, contributing to the antagonism. The leaders of these new churches were accused of being "bandits" unwilling to accept the guidance of the established church and lacking in theological training.

The HChB Synod of November 16-17, 1946, resulted in most member churches changing their name to Huria Kristen Indonesia (HKI), reflecting nationalistic influences in the struggle for Indonesian independence, although a few congregations continue to use the Huria Christen Batak name. When Professor Schepper visited the Bataks in April, 1948, the HKI organized a celebration in his honor, at which time he expressed great disappointment that the HKI had not rejoined the HKBP, especially since the foreigners had now been removed from power. In November, 1948, Dr. Fredrik Schiotz and Bishop Sandegren visited the HKBP as representatives of the LWF and also expressed surprise that the

---

60 Johannes Rauws, et al., The Netherlands Indies, p. 121.

HKI and HKBP were separated even though they shared the same confessional doctrines and the original justification for schism had been eliminated. Schiotz and Sandegren were approached by the HKI Ephorus, who then represented about a hundred thousand members, with a request for Bibles and hymnals. The HKBP and HKI were urged to unite and seek reconciliation. Ephorus Sihombing of the HKBP promised to share Bibles and hymnals received from abroad with the HKI on a proportionate basis, and both groups declared their willingness to seek reconciliation.

Later, Pendeta K. Sirait of the HKBP in Laguboti formed a committee for reconciliation composed of three men each from the HKBP, HKI, Mission Batak, HChB and PKB, but their efforts were unsuccessful. The HKBP had excommunicated everyone who left the HKBP in 1928. Prior to reconciliation the HKBP required that HKI members make open confession of their sin. But many HKI members who had joined since the schism did not consider themselves responsible for what had happened in the past and refused to consider any such confession. Conditions were further complicated by dissension and division in the HKI itself.

The divisions within the HKI tended to divide loyalties between leadership in Pematang Siantar and leadership in Tarutung. The Tarutung group had a larger church and more adequate school system, so they were dissatisfied that the church headquarters should be in Pematang Siantar, even though this was more centrally located for HKI constituent members. Tarutung had tried to have the headquarters moved in several of the Synod meetings, and finally in the Synod meeting of 1962 the Tarutung group separated from the Pematang Siantar group. In August, 1964, representatives from these two groups met at Patane Porsea as a "Committee of Goodwill for the Unity of the HKI," where reconciliation within the HKI was discussed. The committee decided to hold a Synod from September 29 to October 1, 1964, in Medan, where new leaders would be elected for all HKI congregations. Following reconciliation within the HKI, relations with the

HKBP also improved. A joint Pendeta's Refresher Course in 1965 and 1966, the agreement to allow HKI theological students to enter the HKBP seminary at Nommensen University, and the practice of pulpit fellowship indicate the extent of present cooperation.

The HKI is proud that before the War they had private schools with every church, three hundred in number, which ran without government subsidy. These were primary level schools, although about one-half of them used the Dutch language. The HKI now has about forty primary schools, thirteen middle schools, one high school, one technical middle school, and one teacher-training school. A Sekolah for evangelists opened in February, 1967, but is now in financial difficulty. The HKI trained their own pendeta in Pematang Siantar, using headquarters staff and city pastors in a short course for pendeta and congregational teachers. At the present time they have five students studying at Nommensen Department of Theology.

The HKI now numbers 225,000 members in 442 congregations, with 77 pendeta and 5 seminary students. During 1965 alone the HKI increased by 756 adults and 5,750 children. The membership is concentrated around Pematang Siantar and North Tapanuli. The HKI, in November 1967, followed the HKBP and GKPS into the Indonesian Council of Churches (DGI), reaffirming their doctrinal and confessional unity with one another. While they use Luther's *Small Catechism* they have never officially accepted the HKBP's doctrinal statement. They have received some foreign aid through the LWF on the basis of their former relationship with the HKBP and have contacted the RMG about the possibility of establishing a relationship.

The other groups that separated from the HKBP continue to exist. The Mission Batak has five congregations: one in Medan, two in Pematang Siantar, and one each in Tebing Tinggi and Padang Sidempuan. The PKB, which developed in urban areas such as Palembang, Djakarta, and Medan, has seven congregations. In addition there are several other independent congregations scattered throughout Batakland.[61]

---

[61] Andar Lumbantobing, "The Confession of the Batak Church," *op. cit.*, p. 128. Other sources used for the section on the HKI include L. Lumbantobing, "Gerakan Pemuda Kristen Indonesia ditanah Batak dalam hubungan perdjuangan kemerdekaan," in *Pesta Jubeleum 100 Taon Hakristenon di Tano Batak* (Tarutung, September 1, 1961). Also M. H. Pohan, "Pergolakan Pada H. K. I." (typescript).

V

SOCIAL ISSUES AMONG NATIONAL CHURCHES IN BATAKLAND

THE EXPERIENCE OF OLDER WESTERN CHURCHES HAS BEEN OF limited usefulness in relation to contemporary problems facing national churches in North Sumatra. The Batak churches have drawn both from their own indigenous traditions and from their experiences as a mission field to confront social and religious issues in contemporary Indonesian society. As the largest and strongest of the Batak churches, the HKBP has frequently been assigned leadership responsibility in confronting these issues. Several more prominent issues will illustrate the contemporary context.

First, there is political involvement. Whenever possible, the HKBP and other Indonesian churches have refrained from political involvement as churches. But disengagement was not always possible or even desirable. Each political crisis demanded a creative interpretation of doctrine and social responsibility. Second, there is the issue of ecumenical cooperation. While the HKBP strongly supported ecumenical activity among Indonesian churches, it has actively opposed organizational merger with those churches, seeking to preserve its own ethnic and confessional identity. The HKBP has been widely and unjustly condemned for being parochial in its denominational exclusivism. Third, there is higher education. The HKBP has established a large university with secular as well as religious disciplines, serving Muslim and Christian students, earning high respect for its academic credentials throughout Indonesia. Involvement in higher education was a natural development from the system of parochial education in the HKBP and other Batak churches, but the idea has not received unanimous acceptance by either the Bataks or the mission societies. Fourth, there is the problem of schism. Disharmony has plagued the new national churches, vividly evident in the schismatic formation of the GKPI largely out of HKBP membership. This same disharmony, however, is a sign of dynamic vitality and commitment among a dedicated and devout people. Fifth, there is the new relationship of independent churches with foreign missionary organizations. In defining the new relationship to these foreign organizations the national churches have reexamined the relevance and basis of that relationship. Sixth, there is the problem of mass conversion. The mass conversion of Karo Bataks has threatened to engulf the smaller Karo Batak church and has flooded the churches of North Sumatra beyond their capacity to instruct and baptize the new members.

1. POLITICAL INVOLVEMENT

When the German missionaries were interned the morning of May 10, 1940, both Batak Christians and missionaries were forced to accept an autonomous and independent HKBP. The transition was surprisingly smooth. There was immediate chaos throughout the HKBP, "but by the following Sunday the difficulties had been surmounted. The work had been redivided and the Batak ministers took additional duties upon their shoulders so that they now took care of what had formerly been handled by the missionaries."[1]

During the Japanese occupation poverty was universal throughout Batakland and substitutions were found for essential goods. Clothing was made from tree bark or grass fibers, the margins of book pages were used for writing, and some of

---

[1] H. F. de Kleine, *Christ Is the Victor*, p. 8.

the infrequent cars were redesigned to burn wood instead of gasoline. Other substitutions were necessary as well. Many of the laws were changed by the Japanese, who attempted to popularize cults of Japanese culture. Christians were forced to work on Sunday and prohibited from teaching religion or singing hymns in the schools. Some of the church buildings were turned into animal stables. One pendeta with ragged trousers and robe worn to shreds, "was forced to enter the pulpit before the members arrived and asked everyone to leave the church before he was willing to descend."[2]

Very little has been written about church life during the war years in Indonesia. There was little time or energy for introspection. During those times Christianity was stigmatized as a Western religion of the colonialist enemy and barely tolerated by the Japanese. This opposition united Batak Christians behind their own leaders in a spirit of cooperation that caused the membership to grow steadily larger in spite of all difficulties. The spirit of cooperation and the necessity of mutual interdependence crossed boundaries of confessional doctrine and clan loyalties. Plans to build or expand were immediately abandoned when foreign assistance was eliminated and the Christians were forced to depend exclusively and absolutely on one another and the faith they shared.

With the end of the War came the beginning of violent revolution. The Dutch and foreign missionaries, who were released from internment camps, were reluctant to resume their old responsibilities in consideration for the Batak Christians. "Otherwise their Mohammedan countrymen might accuse the Bataks of siding with the Dutch in this struggle for independence."[3] They did not even dare to attend Batak worship services, lest the suspicion of the Muslims be aroused. Missionary de Kleine, later joined by Missionary G. Bos, decided to work among Batak prisoners captured by the Dutch and British forces who had liberated Sumatra. Most of the Batak pendeta had fled to territory occupied by the Republic.

---

[2] Ds. P. T. Sarumpaet, "Kristus Adalah Evangelium Dalam Kesulitan," *Seratus Tahun Kekristenan Dalam Sedjarah Rakjat Batak,* 1961, p. 64.

[3] de Kleine, *op. cit.,* p. 29.

Many Bataks who had previously rejected or ignored the church turned to it in this crisis. Pendeta Henoch Siahaan describes the extent of this movement. "Coming Sunday, I must go to a congregation where 150 people have declared themselves ready to be baptized. The following Sunday I will baptize 50 in another congregation. The next Sunday 200 will be taken into the Congregation of Christ. And then a week later I will hold a mass baptism of 500."[4]

In the Second Police Action, the Dutch invaded Tapanuli on December 23, 1948, the day before Christmas. All attempts to continue programs of social action and education were abandoned. The seminary at Sipoholon, which had been used by the Japanese as a training center but reopened temporarily after the War, was again closed; and the sixty Bible teachers, twenty-six who had families, were forced to abandon their work. The Dutch guarded the roads and roving bands of guerillas occupied the countryside. In the beginning of 1949 many villages, churches, and schools were burned both by the Dutch and the guerillas. Finally, on December 27, 1949, came the armistice and a chance to rebuild.

The HKBP and other Batak churches have existed in a context of violent political turmoil since their independence. In the constitution of the Indonesian state, the five principles of Pantjasila, and especially the first of these principles, have guided the political views of the church. The first principle of *Ketuhanan jang Maha Esa* (Belief in One God) is mentioned in the confession of the HKBP and is interpreted to mean that religious liberty in Indonesia has been guaranteed. It is not considered to mean that monotheistic religion has been established by the state but rather that only God is Lord. Otherwise the state would have to choose between a Triune-God Christianity and Islam, or develop a new super-monotheism. Rather, "this conception is voiced above all others by the government, because it does not want to give preference to any of the various religions, in order to preserve peace among them."[5] The HKBP is aware of the danger,

---

[4] *Ibid.*, p. 56.

[5] Andar Lumbantobing, "The Confession of the Batak Church," in

recognizing that when "nationalism becomes a religion, however, the church must perform its prophetic task."[6]

While rejecting the view that the state is a religious state, the churches have been cautious in their political pronouncements, although church members have been encouraged actively to pursue their responsibilities as Indonesian citizens. During the uprising of the PRRI (Pemerintah Revolusioner Republik Indonesia) Permesta rebels in Sumatra against the central government, General Nasution called on the religious leaders in the army to condemn the insurrection. This was difficult for the HKBP whose membership was divided in their sympathies for and against the rebel cause. The HKBP sent a clarification of its position to President Sukarno on January 12, 1957, and again on February 19, 1958, "which in essence recommended and requested the Head of our Nation to guard and protect the Nation against all difficulties through the present crisis in a spirit of love according to the basis of religion and the will of God."[7] Later, on May 17, 1958, a letter was sent out to all the congregations warning them to be spiritually sensitive to the political confusion during this time and to depend only on Christ for their protection.[8]

The conflict between Christianized Toba and ancestor-worshiping Karo Bataks "underlies the legal history and course of events in the armed uprisings that occurred in 1957 and 1958, largely under Toba leadership, and which were quelled in great measure by the Karo."[9] The rebels opposed Communism and Sukarno but lacked a positive program. They needed ideals more attractive than regional auton-

---

Vilmos Vajta and Hans Weissgerber, *The Church and the Confessions*, p. 127.

[6] *Ibid.*, p. 134.

[7] T. S. Sihombing, "Dimanakah Geredja Berdiri Pada Masa Ini?", *Panatapan Siala Pangulaon ni HKBP* (Pertjetakan: HKBP, 1958), p. 19.

[8] *Ibid.*

[9] M. A. Jaspan, "Ethnic and Racial Relations in Indonesia," Occasional Paper No. 1, Lembaga Penjelidikan Kemasjarakatan Universiteti Negeri Padjadjaran Sosial Research Centre, Padjadjaran State University, Bandung, December, 1959, p. 8.

omy to justify armed rebellion. Religious appeals were impossible since "to fight for God would be compelling only for Moslems as such or Christians as such, and the rebellion was a Moslem-Christian alliance."[10] While the rebel leaders Sjafruddin and Djambek armed Muslim high school students and youth in the Minangkabau and Mandailing areas, the Christian Batak followers of Simbolon had numerous Bible teachers working among them in the Toba areas. When the rebellion was joined by the radical Darul Islam, the inclination of Christian Bataks to negotiate with Djakarta was significantly accelerated.

Government authority is accepted by Batak Christians as a necessity to guard the public welfare and assure a peaceful life for Indonesian citizens. The ultimate loyalty was, however, religious rather than political. As long as the state does not compel the church to follow its political program or to support the state contrary to the dictates of conscience and Christian responsibility, the churches are willing to pledge complete loyalty. The HKBP Ephorus affirms, however, that "we do not believe that the voice of the nation is the voice of God."[11]

In the struggle between Indonesia and Holland over West New Guinea (Irian Barat), the Department of Religion distributed a prayer for the liberation of West New Guinea to be read in all the churches and mosques. The prayer asked God to stand by the Indonesian people on the issue, that a peaceful solution could be found, that sentiment and nationalistic feeling not be allowed to determine the outcome, and that "the Dutch accept the claim of our people and government, to give back West Irian to the Republic of Indonesia, so that friendly relations between the Dutch and Indonesia might be restored."[12] Following this incident the Pastors' Conference of the HKBP passed a directive that "expressly

---

10 Joseph Fischer, "Universities and the Political Process in Southeast Asia," *Pacific Affairs*, XXXV (Spring, 1963), 38.

11 Sihombing, *op. cit.*, p. 20.

12 Badan Pembina Potensi Karya, Kodam II/Bukit Barisan Urusan Rohani, Agama dan Kantor Urusan Agama, Daerah Tingkat I, Sumatra Utara (Bahagian Kristen), "Special Prayer for West Irian," March 2, 1962.

and emphatically informed the congregations that no announcements of the government were to be read in the congregations unless they had been approved by the Ephor."[13]

However, on August 17, 1964, Indonesian Independence Day, another sermon was distributed to the congregations throughout North Sumatra supporting the confrontation against Malaysia. This sermon, based on Psalm 118:10-15, reminded the congregations that Indonesia was surrounded by ballistic missiles and imperialist forces just as Israel had been surrounded when the Psalmist pleaded that God cut down their enemies. Merely to pray for deliverance would not be enough and church members were urged to be ready for the Lord's command to batter down the enemy, which, as it disrupted social harmony, was also the Lord's enemy. "We must crush all our enemies, externally or internally, who disturb our unity through subversive actions, destroying the welfare of society down to its very roots. Dear friends of religious believers! Are you ready to fight against Satan with all his deceptions?"[14] The sermon was read in several churches throughout North Sumatra following a singing of the Indonesian national anthem.

Both Communism and capitalism are condemned by the HKBP as "children of materialism." In 1956 the HKBP sent a circular announcement to all its congregations with a six-point denunciation of Communism at a time when the Communists were rapidly increasing in power and influence throughout Indonesia. The church flatly rejected Communist teachings, maintaining that there is no salvation except through Christ. The statement went on to repudiate "communistic indoctrination by force, communism's contempt for religion as a drug, its repudiation of the concept that sin is transgression against God, its ignorance of the Bible, its obsession with economic factors, and its belief that man's hope is in the communistic community on earth and not in the life

13Lumbantobing, *op. cit.*, p. 134.

14 Panatia Perajaan Hari Kemerdekaan, Sumatra Utara (Bahagian Kristen), "Sermon for Churches," August 17, 1964.

to come."[15] These are only a few examples of a courageous, if not always consistent, stand adopted by the HKBP as an expression of loyalty to the nation and to their Christian faith.

2. ECUMENICAL COOPERATION

With autonomy, there was a strong movement among the Indonesian churches to unite and minimize religious differences. This ecumenical mood, fostered during the Revolution, led to the formation of an Indonesian Council of Churches (Dewan Geredja-Geredja di Indonesia) whose ultimate goal, in 1950 when it was formed, was a single, united church of Christ in Indonesia. One factor delaying that achievement has been a strong stand by the HKBP against the organizational merger of all Indonesian churches.

The 1956 Great Synod of the HKBP discussed the problem of ecumenical unity for Indonesian churches. This Synod came up with a six-point argument against immediate merger. First, they held that there are great differences between the churches in Indonesia. Second, there is visible evidence that ecumenical interaction can take place through existing organizational relationships. Third, this interaction would be facilitated if the DGI remained a council rather than a church. Fourth, the churches of Indonesia are unwilling to give up their newly won autonomy. Fifth, the decisions of the DGI should not be implemented before receiving complete approval of member churches. Sixth, the member churches have already established their own theological schools, while also sending students to the Higher Theological School (Sekolah Theologia Tinggi) in Djakarta.[16] The HKBP preferred that the DGI remain a council and thereby symbolize a high ideal of cooperation for its independent member churches.

The 1964 meeting of the Indonesian Council of Churches in Djakarta followed the theme "Jesus Christ: The Good Shepherd," with a subtheme "The Role of the Church in the Indonesian Revolution." One of the primary questions dis-

---

15 Editorial, *The Christian Century*, LXXIII, 24 (June 13, 1956), 717.

16 Ds. S. Marantika, "Anugerah Dan Karunia Dari Kelimpahan Tuhan" (Djakarta, June, 1960), p. 4.

cussed was that of ecumenical unity. Pendeta G. M. Siahaan, Secretary General of the HKBP, affirmed in a presentation to the assembly that ecumenism is essential to the Christian church as a basic doctrine, although there are different interpretations of that ecumenical imperative. Unity must be an applied, not merely ascribed, activity of the visible, not merely the invisible, church.

Citing examples of ecumenical activity in the HKBP, Pendeta Siahaan indicated the recognized validity of baptism by other churches, acceptance of members from other churches, pulpit fellowship for preaching the Word and administering the sacraments, and interdenominational cooperation often superior to that demonstrated by older churches in Europe or America. While there have been disagreements between the HKBP and other churches, their mutual relationship of cooperation has been maintained. Ecumenical unity is not defined, Siahaan goes on to say, by organizational unity, rules and regulations, liturgical similarity or confessional commonality, but in spiritual fellowship. While the organizational indicators of cooperation contribute to ecumenism they are insufficient to define the ideal of church unity.

Other visible signs of ecumenicity were evident in the DGI. First, member churches from throughout Indonesia were able to gather in fellowship through the DGI. Second, churches were able to exchange ideas, compare problems, and assist one another in solving church and social difficulties. Third, many organizations and institutions, publications, programs of religious education and military chaplaincy, and the increased use of the Indonesian language throughout Indonesian churches demonstrate ecumenicity. Fourth, pastoral meetings and ecumenical services on church holidays have heightened interdenominational cooperation. Fifth, the DGI has been able officially to represent Indonesian churches at international conferences. Sixth, the DGI has been able to assist individual member churches solve their intra- and interchurch problems. Seventh, the DGI has been able to represent member churches to the Indonesian government and society. Eighth, the DGI has been able to facilitate visa applications and distribution of assistance from abroad among member churches more effectively than the individual churches themselves.

The HKBP supported all of these ecumenical activities. In order to continue this activity Pendeta Siahaan recommended that the DGI be strengthened as a council, rather than changed to become a church, establishing regional branches throughout Indonesia. In this way the ecumenical spirit could be disseminated from Djakarta, allowing the member churches and their congregations to experience direct cooperation with other Indonesian Christians. This would increase the contact between the DGI and member-church congregations, allowing the DGI to participate in congregational fellowship more frequently than was possible from Djakarta. Third, the work of the DGI is not limited to Djakarta but also needed in the regions, working through the government and other organizations there. While such regional offices had been established for some time they were inactive for lack of personnel and finances and had virtually died out.

When the HKBP Great Synod of 1951 adopted a Confession of Faith, preparatory to applying for membership in the LWF, this was assumed to contradict and obstruct ecumenical activity. None of the other Indonesian churches has adopted such a confessional statement, but they rather accept the Bible as the Word of God and Jesus Christ as Lord, in a simple statement of their faith. Pendeta Soedarmo from the Geredja Kristen Djawa Tengah (Church of Central Java) reported to the DGI that it would be a mistake to consider the HKBP a Lutheran Church. While the Confession contained many Protestant and Lutheran elements in proclaiming the true Word, recognizing the sacramental validity of baptism and Holy Communion, and church doctrine not unique to Lutheranism, the only uniquely Lutheran element was in their understanding of the sacrament. Pendeta Soedarmo did not discover any basic theological principle in the Confession that would seriously obstruct ecumenical activity between the HKBP and other Indonesian churches.

Before applying to the LWF for membership, the HKBP, pendeta, and congregations discussed the Augsburg Confession, article by article, for two years before concluding that this confession included many references foreign to the Batak context and failed to include problems vital to the HKBP. They then decided to design their own confession of faith. The HKBP Confession was based on classical confessional documents such as the Augsburg Confession and the Heidelberg Catechism. The Barmen Declaration was influential in guiding political involvement by the HKBP. The primary influence was the Batak context in which the HKBP was nurtured, with specific problems of apostasy, syncretism, sectarianism, and ecumenical cooperation being foremost. The Confession responded to the apostolic imperative, separated true from false doctrine, provided a standard of unity for the HKBP, and developed a heritage for future generations. The Confession spoke directly to non-Christian religions, sectarianism within the church, as well as political-social involvement outside the church. The Confession's primary utility lies in the relationship between the HKBP and other churches. The document has been used sparingly if at all in the congregations, teaching institutions, and homes of HKBP members, but has been extremely useful in communication between churches.

Besides the doctrinal arguments for ecumenical unity there were important nontheological justifications. During this time there had been a growing dissatisfaction within many of the Indonesian churches, resulting in schisms and organizational breakdown. The government favored unity as a step toward more harmonious relations in the theological as well as social sectors of the Christian community. Islam was rapidly gaining strength against Communism, and it was thought that a unified church would be able to exert greater influence on society than could the disunited churches. The HKBP, however, felt that compromise on issues of their confession, language, and culture would be impossible for their members at this time. The influence of the HKBP was greater as a member of the council than it would be in a unified church. Without the support of the HKBP immediate plans for the merger of DGI churches are unlikely to succeed.

3. UNIVERSITAS HKBP NOMMENSEN

In November, 1950, the seminary at Sipoholon was reopened on a permanent basis, with financial assistance from the LWF and RMG to rebuild and repair. In a report by Dr. John Gronli to the Commission on Younger Churches and Orphaned Missions, the school at Sipoholon was described as more of a preparatory school than a seminary. The high school at Sipoholon began the second semester of 1951 with 438 pupils, which, together with the enrollment in the teachers' training course and the theological courses, made a total enrollment at Sipoholon of 616 persons plus 300 children enrolled in the day school. There was dormitory space for only five hundred students so facilities were overcrowded, making adequate discipline and sanitation difficult.

> To make the Seminary at Sipoholon what it ought to be it will be necessary: (a) either to separate the High School altogether from the Theological and Teachers' Departments and move the High School to, for instance, Tarutung; (b) or if this involves too great a financial loss because of losing the government grant for the High School, a new dormitory and a new classroom building for the Theological and Teachers' classes should be built some distance away from the present buildings so as to assure enough room and quietness for study. There is plenty of ground belonging to the school at Sipoholon. At present the students are terribly hampered for lack of dormitory space, lack of reading room space for study and especially lack of light, as the present electrical plant does not give nearly enough light to study by.[17]

A serious problem in the HKBP was the shortage of pendeta. By 1955 there were only 134 pendeta for nearly a thousand congregations, with twenty-three other pendeta engaged in

---

[17] John E. Gronli, Report of Dr. Gronli Covering Observations in the Batak Church in 1951, Sumatra, December 28, 1951, Exhibit Indonesia, CYCOM, National Lutheran Council, February 15, 1952, Agenda.

administrative duties.[18] Although most of the pastoral duties in smaller congregations are attended to by religious teachers, evangelists, Bible women, and elders, the shortage of ordained men has continued to pose a problem even today. By 1964 there were still only 220 pendeta to serve 1,300 congregations and 800,000 members, with the membership continuing to increase at a faster rate than ordained pendeta to serve the church could be made available.

The original plans for a university in North Sumatra were begun in 1948, although not formalized by the Synod of the HKBP until 1952. The plan received enthusiastic support by the Great Synod and a preparatory committee was formed to work out details. The committee was made up of well-known Batak leaders, "including the Vice-President of the Parliament, General Secretary of the Ministry of Education, Vice-Governor of Sumatra, Commander-in-Chief of the Armed Forces in Sumatra, and other leaders."[19] The proposals of this committee were unanimously adopted by the Great Synod in 1953.

The Executive Committee of CYCOM was less enthusiastic about the forthcoming university and indicated their concern in a letter to Dr. Arne Bendtz, LWF representative in Sumatra. Dr. Bendtz was informed that if "any anticipation in such discussions that help to provide a university will be supplied by the LWF, it would be well to discourage such thinking."[20] The Secretary of CYCOM learned in May, 1954, that the HKBP planned to open Nommensen University in the fall of that year. Out of concern for rumors that the LWF had promised the HKBP a university, a consultation was immediately held with representatives of the Dutch Missionary Council and a second consultation scheduled for Chicago during the World Council of Churches Assembly.

At the Chicago consultation Batak representatives expressed

---

[18] Winburn Thomas, "Indigenous Batak Church Hopeful," *Christian Century*, October 26, 1955, p. 1254.

[19] The Preparatory Committee of Nommensen University, Pematang Siantar, Sumatra, Indonesia, CYCOM, National Lutheran Council, Exhibit D, Indonesia, Agenda, October 19-20, 1954, p. 37.

[20] CYCOM, National Lutheran Council, Agenda, Indonesia, March 24, 1953, p. 30.

their feelings of urgent need for a Christian university in North Sumatra. The government, Muslim community, and Roman Catholics were all considering new universities, and government permission for such a project was becoming difficult to secure. Dr. Bendtz indicated that the Islamic university at Medan was negotiating with the Rockefeller Foundation for a grant of two million dollars and was receiving favorable consideration as a counterweight to Communism. Baron von Tuyll mentioned the danger that the HKBP would be unable to support both a university in Sumatra and the Christian University and Seminary at Djakarta.[21] However, the HKBP indicated its continuing strong desire to support the Djakarta institution. There was some concern in the Batak community that their students would not be adequately cared for in Djakarta. The Commission finally recognized the need for a Christian institution of higher education in Sumatra, the urgency to implement such a program while government permission was still available, and the need to cooperate closely in this venture with the DGI and the Christian University in Djakarta.[22]

The original plan had been to expand the Sipoholon campus to university status. However, when the regional hospital complex for the Harrison and Crossfield plantations with its administrative building and six large hospital wards was made available for purchase in Pematang Siantar, the decision was made to establish the HKBP university in an urban, coastal region rather than the rural setting of Sipoholon. Two of the hospital wards were converted into dormitories and the third into classrooms, making it possible to begin classes the fall of 1954. On October 7, 1954, the Universitas HKBP Nommensen was founded.[23]

---

[21] Consultation on the Proposed Batak Christian University, Chicago Theological Seminary, August 12, 1954, CYCOM, National Lutheran Council, Exhibit D, Indonesia, Agenda, October 19-20, 1954, p. 43.

[22] *Ibid.*, p. 45.

[23] Lothar Schreiner, "Hospital to Theological Seminary: Nommensen University," *Lutheran World*, V, 1 (June, 1958), 89; also Andar Lumbantobing, "Universitas HKBP Nommensen," *South East Journal of Theology*, I, 1 (July, 1959), 53-56.

The Sekolah Pendeta and Sekolah Theologia Menengah were transferred from Sipoholon to the Nommensen complex and new departments of Theology, Law, and Economics were opened. The students in Sekolah Theologia, who had graduated from the equivalent of junior high school, pursued five years of study followed by three months of field work or more. The students at the new Theological Faculty had graduated from a teachers' training seminary or possessed a university matriculation certificate. Their five years of education included the study of Greek and Hebrew with biblical exegesis in the original biblical languages. The students at Sekolah Pendeta, however, consisted of married primary school teachers who had been serving congregations and had experience in preaching and teaching prior to their three-year course of study at Nommensen.[24]

With such a wide divergence in age and training among the students, there were many problems organizing the curriculum. Each class or year of students had its own schedule, with a fixed number of lectures and courses varying from fourteen to twenty-six required class hours per week.[25] Although the leading staff members of Nommensen were pendeta or members of the HKBP, many foreign staff were also required for the various departments or "faculties." The foreign staff consisted of members drawn from the LWF, the RMG, the Methodist Church, and several Dutch businessmen from Medan. During the first difficult years the leadership of Rector T. S. Sihombing and his successor Dr. Andar Lumbantobing was of critical importance. Also vital was the leadership of Pendeta G. Siahaan as Dean of the Theological Faculty and his successor Pendeta F. Siregar, who, in the vicissitudes of economic, political, and ecclesiastical conflict, demonstrated their courageous adherence to principles of their Christian faith.

The Nommensen theological departments at Pematang Siantar were partially subsidized by the RMG and the LWF, which sent several students to Europe and America for ad-

24 Schreiner, *op. cit.*, pp. 89f.
25 *Ibid.*, p. 90.

vanced theological study as well as providing funds for facilities and running expenses on the Pematang Siantar campus. In 1963 there were three students studying in the United States and four in West Germany. The Theological Faculty is now a member in the Association of Theological Schools in Southeast Asia and is able to offer a recognized Sardjana Muda (B.A.) degree in theology. The library at Nommensen is probably the best in North Sumatra with 12,000 books in the theological library, 5,000 volumes at the Medan campus, and 237 volumes in the Education Department library. The Department of Theology now includes two hundred students with ninety in the first-year class. The sharp increase in enrollment resulted from many non-HKBP students enrolling, particularly from the Karo church.

Because of a shortage in teaching personnel the Law Faculty had to be closed and the Economics Faculty was transferred to Medan in 1957. The Rector of Nommensen, T. S. Sihombing, was soon called to become Secretary General of the HKBP and was replaced by Dr. Andar Lumbantobing. The university took on an ecumenical character with students from the Mentawai Islands, Nias, the Simalungun church, the Methodist Church, and the Karo church.

There were a number of departmental changes in the structure of Nommensen. The Law Faculty was the first to close. Then a Faculty of Engineering was attempted in 1956, but closed due to the expulsion of Dutch citizens who served as instructors. It reopened in November, 1961, but finally closed on July 17, 1963. The Academy of Business Administration and Accounting was started on July 1, 1961, at the Medan Campus and continues today under the title Fakultas Katatalaksanaan Niaga. A Faculty of Mathematics was opened on July 21, 1963, but is not yet operational. In 1962 a Teacher-Training (FKIP) Faculty was opened at Pematang Siantar with a massive building program to erect an assembly hall, cafeteria, dormitories, and faculty housing. By 1963 the program had enrolled 262 students. The funds for this building project were provided by the German government and administered by the RMG.

In 1957, the Ford Foundation began a program of assistance aimed at building up the Economics Faculty in Medan. This assistance included providing seven foreign professors for periods of one or two years each, sending seventeen students from Nommensen to America for advanced degrees, and providing large quantities of textbooks and educational equipment. This project, administered through the National Lutheran Council, had invested about a million dollars building up facilities on the Medan Campus by 1964 when the project was terminated. When the Ford Foundation — National Lutheran Council program of assistance began in September, 1957, there was no full-time teaching staff at Nommensen, nor were there buildings or land. Academic administration was almost exclusively in the hands of part-time foreign employees, experienced in business but not academic affairs. The faculty had rented a building but had no library or books. "The Faculty of Economics was little more than a device to bring together teachers and students, both fully occupied elsewhere, for a number of lectures each week."[26]

In May, 1966, the Ministry of Education granted the Nommensen Department of Economics full recognition for their Sardjana Muda degree and provisional recognition to the Sardjana degree, conditional on an examination held under state supervision. The Sardjana Muda degree is roughly equivalent to the B.A. and the Sardjana degree to an M.A. By the end of 1963 the Economics Faculty had 24 Sardjana graduates, 132 Sardjana Muda graduates, and 411 students who had received the two-year degree of Persiapan. The Business and Accountancy Academy had produced 113 students with the Persiapan degree, and, before closing down, the Engineering Faculty produced 26 students with the Persiapan degree.

Besides Nommensen University, the HKBP established the Sekolah Guru Puteri (Women Teachers' School) at Sipoholon in August, 1955. In 1961, the Perguruan Teknik (Technical

---

26 Douglas Paauw, "The Faculty of Economics: Achievements, Problems and Prospects," in *Universitas HKBP Nommensen Yearbook* (Medan, 1961), p. 79.

School) was established at Pematang Siantar. This vocational school is under the direction of T. H. Hutabarat, assisted by Ir. A. Butsch, Peters, and Hanebuth from Germany. The Rector of the Sekolah Pendeta and Director of Sekolah Guru Huria at Sipoholon is Pendeta K. Lumbantoruan. The Sekolah Bibelvrouw (Bible Women's School) is under the direction of Pendeta K. Sirait.

4. CHURCH SCHISM

A struggle that was to divide the ministerium and membership of the HKBP in 1964 began as a disagreement between the Rectorium (Rector, Vice-President, and Departmental Deans) and the Board of Directors for Nommensen University in 1963. On July 21, 1963, the Nommensen Board of Directors decided first, to raise tuition fees 300 percent at the Medan Campus, making this the principal source of financial support, and second, to allow full-time teaching staff to engage in outside employment. These decisions, which at first affected only the Medan Campus, attempted to solve increasingly critical financial problems by putting the university on a self-supporting basis rather than depending on church subsidy. The Rectorium wanted higher faculty salaries and church aid to improve academic standards without raising tuition. The Rectorium consequently decided to require, on their own authority, that full-time faculty withdraw from outside employment and to press for a pay increase.

In defiance of this order, two faculty members distributed mimeographed pamphlets attacking the Rectorium, soliciting support from the student body and the Board of Directors. The Board of Directors responded by taking over financial affairs of the university and asking for the resignation of the Vice-President. The crisis was further escalated when the Rectorium, on September 12, 1963, declared that they no longer recognized the authority of the Board Chairman, a decision widely supported by Nommensen faculty members. On September 20, 1963, the Board of Directors relieved the Rector of his responsibilities and referred the matter to the HKBP hierarchy. On October 15, 1963, the Rectorium retaliated, declaring that they no longer recognized the Ephorus of the Batak church, and appealed their case to the HKBP membership. By the time the HKBP Church Board was able to meet to discuss the problem, the Rector was no longer willing to attend and the position of the Rectorium was condemned by the Church Board.

In sympathy with the Rectorium, a group of HKBP pendeta established a Committee for Reformation and withdrew from the HKBP. This group of dissatisfied pendeta had either been reassigned to other congregations against their wishes or were otherwise opposed to the increased centralization of authority in the HKBP. The church regulations of 1962, which eliminated the district synods and placed directive authority in the Church Board, became a source of dissatisfaction for those members who preferred a more decentralized polity. Also in 1962 the Nommensen Charter was modified with a new set of bylaws, in accord with instructions from the Ministry of Higher Learning and Sciences, making the Political Manifesto of the state the basis of the new charter and placing the university under the direct responsibility of the Nommensen Board of Directors. The new regulations were interpreted as destructive of local autonomy and individual freedom, placing the pendeta and faculty members under the direct control of the church hierarchy.

On October 21, 1963, the Governor of North Sumatra established a temporary Presidium to assume control of the university and enable its continued operation. This enforced cooling off period canceled all decisions made thus far during the dispute and returned to the conditions of July, 1963, in the hope that the parties concerned would be able to settle their dispute privately. When the conflict continued, prominent members of the HKBP formed a Committee for Unity to mediate the argument. But when this attempt was discouraged by the HKBP hierarchy, they sided with the Rectorium and dissident pendeta. There were numerous demonstrations throughout North Sumatra demanding a Special Great Synod to settle the dispute, with a group of dissident pendeta signing a pledge to oppose the HKBP hierarchy regardless of consequences. The government's increasing concern was demonstrated by the Department of Higher Education in Djakarta requesting a full report and the government Presidium prohibiting further public discussion of the problem. Attempts by organizations and individuals from both sides to mediate the dispute seemed actually to accelerate the conflict.

From July 19 to 25, 1964, a Special Great Synod of the HKBP was held at Parapat, attended by a Minister of State (W. J. Rumambi) representing President Sukarno, Secretary General Marantika with a delegation from the Indonesian Council of Churches, and the Governor of North Sumatra. A Special Committee was established with representatives from both sides to negotiate a settlement.

Indonesia was in a state of national emergency due to the confrontation policy against Malaysia, with a tense political climate, regular air raid practices, and constant preparedness for foreign invaders. Furthermore, there was a strong Marxist influence at work in Indonesian society, with some seeking to heighten the church dispute. A similar pattern of conflict was evident in several other churches throughout Indonesia, inspiring the suspicion of Communist involvement. While the government expressed a conviction that the problem was not theological, it maintained a tolerant attitude with little direct involvement.

The church viewed Nommensen as one of its institutions along with many others, dedicated to the role of serving the demands and needs of the community as defined by the church hierarchy. The university, however, saw its role as one of leadership through an intellectual center of learning, to change or reform the social order and not merely to preserve and refine accepted traditional approaches. The church hierarchy was uneasy that the university take too prominent a role in the reforming of society and its institutions. This was the domain of the church and was ultimately a spiritual problem. Intellectual training at a university should rather concentrate on historical subject matters.

The Chairman of the Nommensen Board of Directors, Dr. T. D. Pardede, is a wealthy industrialist who has achieved phenomenal success in business since the Second World War. He sought to apply his own successful business methods to the running of Nommensen University. This involved a hierarchical structure of authority incompatible with the egalitarianism of the dissidents. He resented the Rectorium for assuming too much directive power in establishing policy contrary to the authority of the Board of Directors and the directives of the HKBP. He expressed the conviction that God had sent him to use his talents in guiding the university and was confounded by the Rectorium's ingratitude as he worked toward those ends. This was especially true since he had pursued those changes through legal and constitutional means in the HKBP and Nommensen University.

The Rectorium supported many "international" ideas in the running of their university which attracted criticism from the church as well as the government. Most of the full-time faculty had been educated abroad, most of the library books were in English, and some of the faculty were themselves foreigners. The theological departments at Pematang Siantar and the Economics and Business Administration departments in Medan both had been largely dependent on foreign aid. Some foreign influence was therefore unavoidable, if not desirable. The Rectorium resented the university being reduced to a factory, even a highly efficient factory, and themselves being reduced to employees or "tools" in that factory. They resented the Chairman's formative decisions on educational policy as an intrusion on their authority. When the Ephorus supported the Board of Directors, the Rectorium attacked him as well, "in the interest of the University, the Church and in the name of Truth which must survive in the Church."[27]

Others who also experienced the turmoil of this conflict will recognize the foregoing description as oversimplified and focused on only one dimension of this multifaceted struggle. In order really to understand the nature of the conflict it is perhaps necessary to consider the Batak personality. An influ-

---

27 Andar Lumbantobing, and Drs. H. M. T. Oppusunggu, "Letter of Declaration," October 1, 1963 (typescript).

ential Djakarta Batak layman described the forces involved
as growing out of the Batak character.

> The first element is 'Soul,' Christian, Protestant. The second
> element is 'Blood,' Batak, Progressive. These two active and
> sometimes contradictory forces were united in the Batak Chris-
> tian. Both sides were working toward unity within the HKBP
> in the spirit of serving God through faith, hope and strong
> determination. As each side pursued this goal in a progressive
> and revolutionary way the conflict between them continued
> to grow.[28]

The government, supporting the decisions of the Great
Synod of the HKBP, banned and prohibited organizations
opposed to those decisions. The seven dissident members of
the Special Working Committee, established by church and
government to solve the problem, immediately withdrew, and
negotiations broke down on August 14, 1964. The delegation
of dissidents went to Pematang Siantar to meet with Dr.
Andar Lumbantobing, seeking his support in starting a new
church. Dr. Lumbantobing did not agree with the actions
of this delegation, considering their move toward schism
theologically unjustified. Dr. S. M. Hutagalung, who was also
approached, agreed with Dr. Lumbantobing while at the
same time expressing sympathy for any individual who "felt
his belief and faith and nearness to God was being disrupted."[29] Nonetheless, when the Geredja Kristen Protestant
Indonesia was established at the Salvation Army hall in Pematang Siantar on August 23, 1964, Dr. Lumbantobing and Dr.
Hutagalung, who were not present, were appointed to the
highest positions of leadership.[30] On the basis of their appointment, the HKBP expelled both Dr. Lumbantobing and Dr.
Hutagalung, who then on August 30, 1964, accepted roles of
leadership in the GKPI.

In the original agreement to establish the GKPI the group
ascribed to the same confessional form as the HKBP but

---

28 S. Pandjaitan, *HKBP Berdjoang* (Djakarta, 1964), p. 32.

29 M. C. Togatorup, "Mengheningkan Tjipta Satu Tahun GKPI, 30
Augustus, 1964—30 Augustus, 1965," *Suara GKPI*, August 1, 1965, p. 10.

30 *Ibid.*

established its own polity and organization. The group also expressed its willingness to dissolve and return to the HKBP, "as soon as the HKBP comes back to the basis of its belief in a true understanding of the Church."[31] When the charter of the GKPI was established, on October 31, 1964, the doctrinal position of the HKBP was reaffirmed. The GKPI declared its foundation to be the Old and New Testament and Jesus Christ as King of the church. The GKPI acknowledged as its creed a belief in the Apostolicum and Luther's *Small Catechism* as a true interpretation of the Bible.[32]

The GKPI drew members from many tribes and regions of North Sumatra, although the majority of its membership came from the Toba Bataks in the HKBP. Beginning with seven congregations on August 30, 1964, the group had grown to 188 congregations and to 54,127 members, of which fifty-nine have been converted from Islam, 166 have been converted from ancestor worship, and 53,127 have come from other churches.[33] By 1966 the GKPI had 195 congregations and 65,000 members.

5. NATIONAL CHURCH AND FOREIGN MISSIONS

Classifications intended to differentiate between churches of the nineteenth century who sent missionaries and churches of the twentieth century who received them have been singularly unsuccessful. The ideas of old or young, Western or Eastern, have frequently served as vague impressions on which to hang conventional preconceptions, prejudices, and characterizations. Ephorus T. S. Sihombing of the HKBP rightly condemns those who depend on these categories, for whom "the term 'national' or 'younger churches' means the same as 'weak and backward,' the term 'European or older churches' means 'strong and dominant.' "[34] The difference, insofar as it

31 M. C. Simandjuntak, "Mengheningkan Tjipta," *Suara GKPI*, September 1, 1965, p. 8.

32 Andar Lumbantobing, "GKPI Genap Dua Tahun," *Suara GKPI*, August 30, 1966, p. 8.

33 "Perkembangan GKPI," *Suara GKPI*, August 30, 1966, p. 38.

34 T. S. Sihombing, "Partnership Between Mission and National and European Churches" (Pematang Siantar, June 11, 1966), p. 1.

exists, is not theological but geographical, social, and historical. Frequently, "the oriental knows the western man as the unwelcome foreigner who is impatient, domineering, fearsome and who in appearance and behavior completely differs from himself."[35]

In its proper perspective the relationship is not one of independence but of interdependence, not between younger and older churches but of universal church. "True Christian interdependence is betrayed not only by paternalistic relationships, but also when those who wish to reject paternalism — be they in East or West — act and speak as if they could stand apart, when they say to one another: We have no need of you."[36] The Ephorus continues to speak directly to the Western missionary when he says, "You are not autonomous in this part of the world either. None are autonomous, and international agencies, in particular, must remember that they are bound by the wisdom that has come from international conferences."[37]

When the foreign missionary organizations returned to Indonesia after the Second World War they affirmed the vitality of the indigenous church and the ability of their leaders. The RMG acknowledged that after the first shock caused by the internment of the missionaries, the life of the church went on hardly interrupted by the absence of the European workers. The relationship between the now independent HKBP and the RMG was officially recognized by Pendeta T. S. Sihombing in 1946, and later, in 1948, when Pendeta K. Sitompul attended a meeting of the LWF in Germany requesting rights to RMG property in Batakland. The Continental Mission Conference at Bremen in 1920 had unanimously declared that all mission property on the fields was destined for the younger churches and would never be reclaimed. The RMG, which concurred in that decision, reaffirmed its position on November 13, 1946, regarding mission property in North Sumatra. The property had been con-

35 *Ibid.*, p. 2.
36 *Ibid.*, p. 10.
37 *Ibid.*, p. 14.

fiscated first by the Japanese and then by the Indonesian
Republic, but there was hope that the property could be
transferred through the Mission Consulate in Batavia on the
Dutch-occupied east coast and through the Republic for the
remaining properties. The RMG left no doubt as to the
HKBP's rightful claim in this matter.

> The Deputation of the Rhenish Mission Society herewith
> declares that the whole Rhenish Mission property in Sumatra
> is belonging to the HKBP. This property includes all pieces
> of ground and buildings, which have been gained or built
> by money of the Rhenish Mission in Sumatra, further, all
> pieces of ground and buildings, which have been gained or
> built in its leading by the help of the legal assistance of the
> government.[38]

The Mission Consul planned to transfer the property to the
HKBP as soon as a peace treaty with Germany would be
signed, assuming this as the intent of the Dutch government
in confiscating the property in the first place. The sympathy
of the Mission Consulate was clearly with the HKBP. "Neither the Government nor the Batak Church wishes the return
of the Rhenish Mission as an organization in Indonesia."[39]
The Mission Consulate expressed the hope that any German-
born missionaries returning to work among the Bataks come
either through non-German missionary organizations or under
the framework of the indigenous church. The later harmonious relationship between the RMG and the Batak churches,
as well as with the foreign missionary organizations, completely failed to confirm these postwar anxieties. During the
summer of 1950 the RMG missionary Dr. Müller-Krüger,
professor at the Higher Theological School at Djakarta,
traveled through Tapanuli and enjoyed warm fellowship
with the Batak church leaders. The HKBP conveyed a request

[38] Excerpt from the Minutes of a meeting between officers of the
Rhenish Mission Society and Ds. Sitompul and Ds. Siregar for the HKBP
held at Barmen, Germany, October 1, 1948, CYCOM, National Lutheran
Council, Agenda, Exhibit D, Indonesia, December 2, 1949, pp. 7-8.

[39] The Missionconsuls in Indonesia, Zendingsconsulaat, Van Heutz-
boulevard 17, Batavia, August 10, 1948, Exhibit J, CYCOM, National
Lutheran Council, December 2, 1949.

for three physicians and several nurses through him to the RMG, reestablishing a relationship of harmonious cooperation.

LWF involvement with the HKBP grew out of friendly relations between the delegation from the HKBP and the Tamil Evangelical Lutheran Church of South India at the Tambaram meeting of the International Missionary Council in 1938. After the War the Tamil Lutherans discussed the possibility of sending aid to Indonesia, helping the German missions there as they had in India. After discussions with Dr. Ralph Long of the National Lutheran Council, Bishop Johannes Sandegren of the Tamil Lutheran Church visited Djakarta in the late spring of 1947. With meticulous care for ecumenical relationships, he discussed plans with the Anglican and Methodist Bishops in Singapore, the Dutch Mission Consuls in Batavia (Djakarta), and missionaries Gramberg of Oegstgeest and de Kleine of the RMG before meeting with eighteen Batak church leaders who cautiously agreed to initiate contact between Bishop Sandegren and the Ephorus of the HKBP. Because of the Police Action between the Dutch and the Republic, Bishop Sandegren was only able to send a letter to the Ephorus via courier before returning to India.[40] In early 1948 the Dutch Mission Council, after unsuccessfully soliciting help from the Presbyterian Church (USA), turned to the Commission on Younger Churches and Orphaned Missions of the National Lutheran Council in the United States for assistance to the Bataks. For political reasons the Dutch were unable to give direct aid to the Bataks. At about the same time the RMG missionaries in South China who were receiving help from CYCOM inquired from Dr. Daniel Nelson if similar assistance could be provided to the HKBP.[41]

The HKBP was reluctant to establish relations with German or Dutch missions on the same basis as before the War because of a desire to protect their newly won autonomy.

---

[40] Fredrik A. Schiotz, "Lutheran World Missions," *International Review of Missions*, XLIII (1954), 311-322.

[41] *Ibid.*, p. 316.

Bishop Sandegren felt an Indian missionary would be appropriate as a fellow Asian from another emerging, independent nation and in view of the long historical tradition of interaction between India and Sumatra. Dr. D. R. Williams was sent by the LWF through the Tamil church as a medical missionary to assist the HKBP, arriving at HKBP headquarters in Tarutung on March 30, 1948. Dr. Williams set up a medical relief unit in the name of the LWF near Balige, with twelve assistants supervising four other medical clinics in the Toba region. The only other HKBP doctor was Dr. H. L. Tobing, who was later killed by the Dutch, and there was an enormous amount of work. Dr. Williams wrote, "I should mention here that I am the only doctor in a district where there are 3 sub-hospitals, 12 dispensaries, 1 leper asylum (of 230 patients) and an infirmary for the crippled and the blind."[42]

Several months later Dr. Williams conveyed a request from the Ephorus concerning HKBP membership in the LWF and requesting a visit from LWF representatives to Sumatra. After this request was discussed at the IMC-NLC meeting in Amsterdam in August, 1948, it was agreed that Bishop Sandegren and Dr. Fredrik A. Schiotz would visit the Batak church. In September Dr. Schiotz met with several representatives of the HKBP attending the Missionstag of the German Evangelical Missionary Council at Herborn, and later with representatives of the RMG who advised "a friendly caution against the unwise provision of help, lest it become a means of robbing a young church of its real autonomy."[43]

Traveling through the Dutch lines into Republic territory, Bishop Sandegren and Dr. Schiotz visited the Bataks in November, 1948, against the advice of the Dutch intelligence service. In conversation with the Church Board of the HKBP a request was made for one American and one Indian theological professor and material assistance in the form of a car,

---

[42] Dr. D. R. Williams, Letter to the Secretary of Lutheran World Federation, New York, USA, May 22, 1948, CYCOM, National Lutheran Council, Agenda, 1949.

[43] Schiotz, op. cit., p. 317.

Bibles, and hymnals. These requests were relayed to the CYCOM. In response to inquiries about membership in the LWF it was suggested that this possibility be discussed among the districts of the HKBP and then formal application be made before the LWF Assembly in 1952. The HKBP cabled a request for membership to Dr. Schiotz in December, 1948. While in Sumatra Bishop Sandegren and Dr. Schiotz were also approached by the Simalungun church and the Indonesian Protestant Church (HKI) for aid, but suggested that all requests be forwarded through the HKBP.[44]

Other international organizations were also in contact with the HKBP. In 1949 the General Secretary of the World Council of Churches, Dr. Visser 't Hooft, and the Secretary of the IMC, Dr. Charles W. Ranson, visited the HKBP. "A great amount of money was offered as assistance to the Batak Church. This offer was turned down by the Batak Church. They pointed to the fact that receipt of such funds would be irregular in view of the fact that the Church was in the process of negotiation with LWF."[45] Also, Professor Dr. Schepper, President of the Netherlands Missionary Council, visited Sumatra in April, 1948, "with a view to sound the general feeling in the Batak Church towards receiving some Dutch missionaries and others."[46]

Dr. Williams was suspicious of the conciliatory attitude by the Dutch government toward the HKBP, offering them back their schools and hospitals in an attempt to win their political support. "When the Batak Church is won the Batak Christians are won; when the Batak Christians are won the population of Tapanuli is as good as won as it is in a Christian majority; and when that is achieved a puppet state of Tapanuli is born."[47] The HKBP was not in a financial position to run the institutions should they be returned, forc-

---

[44] Bishop J. Sandegren and Fredrik A. Schiotz, "Visit Among the Bataks," November, 1948 (typescript).

[45] N. Arne Bendtz, "Faith of the Batak," *Frontiers*, XII, 5 (January, 1961), 20.

[46] Dr. D. R. Williams, *op. cit.*

[47] Dr. D. R. Williams to Rev. Dr. J. Sandegren, Letter of April 11, 1949, CYCOM, National Lutheran Council, Agenda, 1950.

ing them to seek assistance perhaps through Dutch government subsidy, implying their recognition of Dutch authority.

An application by the HKBP was placed before the LWF executive meeting in Oxford, July, 1949, where it was decided to meet with HKBP representatives. In view of the "reported deep concern in Barmen over the HKBP's application for membership in the LWF," it was decided that a meeting between the LWF delegation and representatives from the RMG would precede the scheduled meeting with Bataks at Trichinopoly.[48] The Commission promised, "There will be no coercion or manipulation exercised at Trichinopoly; but even as due consideration will be given to the Rhenish Society's point of view as far as it may be germane, so also the same consideration will have to be given to the Batak attitude."[49] There was much concern among the Dutch Missionary Council, the IMC, the German Missionary Council, and the RMG that the HKBP's admission into LWF would jeopardize their relationship with other Indonesian churches in the Indonesian Council of Churches, which was then being formed. Many Indonesian churches were afraid that this move would isolate the HKBP confessionally, inhibiting their participation in the Indonesian Council of Churches and ultimate membership in an Indonesian Union Church. Other attempts were made to prove the strong Reformed influences in Batak church doctrine. When Pendeta Sitompul and Ds. Siregar met with officers of the RMG in Barmen on October 1, 1948, Dr. E. Verwiebe expressed his disapproval of the growing attachment between the HKBP and the LWF.

> For the sake of the inner development and the great task also today it is necessary to abstain from any influence as to the formation of its way. Such influence, however, would unavoidably follow if the Batak-Church joined the Lutheran World Federation and as soon as strictly Lutheran theologians would be sent to the Batak-Church. With regard to the blessing of

---

[48] Agenda, CYCOM, National Lutheran Council, December 2, 1949, p. 12.

[49] *Ibid.*, p. 13.

all the churches of Christ in Indonesia, we must intensely dissuade from such a step and we are grateful to know that the Lutheran brethren today, as formerly the Reformed ones, will be ready to assist the young church helpfully and intercedingly renouncing any influence.[50]

Others in the Dutch Missionary Council and elsewhere concurred in criticism of the LWF, which was accused of doctrinal imperialism while the HKBP was accused of expedient opportunism, seeking financial advantage through international affiliation. While one group of theologians accused the LWF of confessional imperialism and buying churches with promises of financial assistance, another group was accusing the LWF for being latitudinarian and doctrinally indifferent for admitting the HKBP. Pronouncements of CYCOM, F. L. Bakker's articles in *De Heerbaan,* and consequent publications have largely eliminated the misunderstanding on which these accusations were based.

Ephorus Justin Sihombing and former Ephorus Pendeta K. Sirait met with the LWF representatives Bishop Anders Nygren, Bishop Johannes Sandegren, and Dr. F. A. Schiotz at Rajahmundry, India, on January 16-17, 1950. The Batak delegation was under instructions, "to tell this meeting what we think and are, but not to submit to anything new or strange."[51] While the HKBP did not consider itself 100 percent "Lutheran," they felt they were "closer to Lutherans than to anyone else."[52] The LWF representatives cleared up any doubts that as an LWF member the HKBP would be restrained from further ecumenical activity.

Any participation in the LWF should not stand as a barrier for co-operation with other Christian churches, but should rather be a help to further and enrich its fellowship with sister Christian churches. Thus the present co-operation in the Djakarta Theological College, and in the National Coun-

---

[50] Excerpt from the Minutes of a meeting between officers of the Rhenish Mission Society and Ds. Sitompul and Ds. Siregar for the HKBP held at Barmen, Germany, October 1, 1948.

[51] Keith Bridston, "The L. W. F. and the HKBP," n.d. (typescript).

[52] *Ibid.*

cil of Churches in Indonesia, and so forth, should in no way be impaired.[53]

When Pendeta K. Sitompul and Pendeta P. Sarumpaet represented the HKBP at the Hannover Assembly of the LWF in 1952, they brought with them a carefully thought out "Confession of Faith," prepared by a committee of Batak pendeta and adopted by the HKBP Great Synod of November, 1951. On the basis of this confessional statement they were accepted into the LWF.

All financial assistance from the LWF and RMG to the HKBP is directed in its distribution and budgeting by the Committee on Reconstruction and Inter-Church Aid, which includes Batak representatives from each of the major institutions of the HKBP along with representatives from the LWF and the RMG. The Committee on Reconstruction and Inter-Church Aid was assigned to make special surveys and studies regarding the reconstruction and financial needs of the HKBP and formulate these along with requests for interchurch aid and personnel supervising the allocation and distribution of aid. The chairman was designated as the HKBP Ephorus. The members included from three to five members of the church council and a representative of each organization giving permanent help to the HKBP. Regulations were drawn up and adopted by the HKBP Great Synod in 1951.

> The HKBP considers itself responsible for any help which is received from abroad. The aid will be used for the specific purpose for which it has been requested. The Office on Reconstruction will supervise the distribution of the aid in the most efficient way and prepare responsible reports after the distributing has been accomplished. The final responsibility of this Office rests with the Church Council which, however, can appoint executive members of this office from any member of the organizations that participate in this office. Again the Church Council prepares the broad policy to be followed and the Ephorus is empowered to appoint permanent advisers to increase the efficiency of the work of reconstruction.[54]

---

[53] Schiotz, *op. cit.*, p. 319.

[54] A Statement from the HKBP Governing the Function of Its Newly

Besides the LWF, the HKBP also receives assistance from Lutheran World Relief in the form of medical supplies to the Balige and Saribudolok hospitals, thus far totaling $590,-000.[55] The social-work section of the HKBP has further received shipments of clothing and powdered milk from Church World Service via the Commission on Interchurch Aid of the DGI. Currently a HKBP agricultural project is being established at Balige directed by the German agriculturalist, Moulsen, and a Community Development Service representative from Holland was placed in Pematang Siantar in 1969.

The LWF had begun work in Indonesia as an emergency measure following the Second World War to fill a temporary need. For some time persons inside and outside the LWF had questioned the advisability of LWF serving as a source of personnel and missionary assistance to the Batak churches. As a consequence the LWF sent out an invitation in 1967-68 to any church or mission board interested in assuming responsibility for work in Indonesia. The invitation, directed especially to those church organizations already working in Indonesia, drew no immediate response. Finally the HKBP, HKI and GKPS leadership took the initiative and contacted the Lutheran Church in America Board of World Missions, requesting that the LCA accept the LWF invitation. After some study and consideration the LCA/BWM agreed to "assume basic mission responsibilities in Indonesia starting in January, 1970.... "[56] The LWF will continue to work closely with the churches in Indonesia but will no longer serve as an assisting mission body as it has in the past.

6. The Karo Mass Movement to Christianity

The Dutch missionaries were first able to return among the Karo when the area was occupied during the Second Po-

Organized Division on Reconstruction and Inter-Church Aid, CYCOM, National Lutheran Council, Exhibit C, Indonesia, March 24, 1953, p. 1.

55 Ove R. Nielsen, "Indonesia: Staff Field Visit Report," Lutheran World Relief, November 11-18, 1966.

56 *Information,* Lutheran World Federation News Service, Geneva, Release No. 7/69, p. 7, February, 1969.

lice Action. In 1948 missionaries H. Vuurmans, D. Solinger, and H. de Ridder were able to return to work with the Geredja Batak Karo Protestant. In 1940 they had left the Karo church with about five thousand members, a large number of schools, two hospitals with a total of three hundred fifty beds, a leprosarium with three hundred patients, and a hospital for the severely ill. The GBKP had inherited institutional indebtedness far beyond their financial capacity. On April 1, 1948, Dr. M. V. Roolvink-Fransen and Mr. H. Neumann arrived to help reestablish the medical work, and were soon followed by several other doctors, midwives, and nurses. The group received assistance from the Dutch Public Health Service, the Red Cross, several east coast plantations, and private individuals. Missionary N. W. van der Bent arrived to manage the religious bookstore on Djalan Sutomo in Medan in 1955, but was forced by the Indonesian government, as were most Dutch citizens, to leave in 1959. On April 29, 1960, Dr. P. E. Treffers departed as the last medical missionary to the GBKP for the time being.[57]

When the RMG sent their missionary, Werner Grothaus, to work among the Karo in 1963, the church had virtually isolated itself against all foreign missionaries, and about 70 percent of the Karo were neither Muslim nor Christian. By this time there were twenty-three thousand members, eight ordained pendeta, and twenty-two evangelists working under the GBKP. Evangelization was almost entirely in the hands of the lay elders, presbyters, and deacons. The women's organization called Moria would frequently organize evangelistic meetings in the villages. It was then reported: "The Karo Church now has 120 preaching stations in which the Word of God is preached every Sunday. One can say that in 75 percent of all these places the laymen run the services."[58]

For the last decade the Communists had been particularly

---

[57] H. Neumann, Een Korte Nabeschouwing, "Gegevens Over Het Zendingswerk in de Karo-Bataklanden," Oegstgeest Bibliotheek Nederlandse Zendingshogeschool, 1966.

[58] Werner Grothaus, "Ein Volk im Aufbruch auf den guten Weg," *Welt* (March, 1967), pp. 3ff.

active among the Karo, either directly through the Communist Party (PKI) or indirectly through several front organizations. The Communists were always able to find jobs for the unemployed and secure farming materials at a discount for their followers. Many congregations were infiltrated. "There was one congregation, discovered later, where one of the elders was himself a Communist leader and where fifty percent of the members were Communist Party members."[59] Communists were particularly active among the youth, teaching propaganda in the schools during free time allocated for teaching religion.

On October 1, 1965, all Indonesia was terrified to hear that the Communists were making their long-awaited grasp for power, and it was with some relief that the Christian community learned how that attempt failed. The relief was magnified as hidden stores of weapons, Communist flags, and lists of persons to be executed were uncovered. There were more than three thousand persons from Karoland on those lists, including Christians, Muslims, and Buddhist public leaders. Mass graves had already been dug in two places.[60] Groups of Indonesians across the nation rose up in uncontrollable fury, massacring undetermined numbers who had been associated, or accused of being associated, with the Communist Party.[61] Many innocent as well as guilty persons were victimized by self-appointed vigilante groups during this time.

One of the most dramatic and surprising reactions following the abortive 1965 coup is the mass movement of Indonesians into the church. This movement has been especially strong among the Karo Bataks. On April 24, 1966, the Sumatra regional office of the DGI organized an evangelization program for the Karo Batak area. On May 10 a committee of pendeta was appointed to carry on this work, led by A. Ginting Suka, L. Purba, and W. Panggabean. There were

59 *Ibid.*, p. 4.

60 *Ibid.*

61 Frank Cooley, "Reflections on the Massacre of Communists in Indonesia," 1967 (typescript).

twenty-seven others assigned to eight divisions of responsibility within the committee.

The first campaign began on May 28 with an evangelization
team of fifteen hundred Christians led by the North Sumatra
military (Koanda) Commander J. Muskita, the Governor
of North Sumatra, P. R. Telaumbanua, representatives from
the DGI, pendeta from Sumatran churches, brass bands,
choirs, and other Christians. The first village was Tiga Bi-
nanga, followed by a visit on May 29 to Kabandjahe and
Tiga Nderket. Similar mass evangelization teams visited three
other towns in June, one in July, three in August, one in
September, and two in December. In June a team of fifteen
hundred Christians led by fifty-seven pendeta from five
churches in North Sumatra held a meeting in the public
market of Tiga Lingga. The meeting was attended by an
estimated twenty thousand persons, and 1,903 persons were
baptized.[62] In the next few weeks another five hundred were
baptized in a neighboring village as the movement around
Dairi continued to grow. Pendeta Asal Simandjuntak, the
General Secretary of the Sumatra DGI Regional Office, described the evangelization of Munthe on July 7, 1966. "We
started the meeting around 9:30 in the evening, and it lasted
until 1:30 in the morning. There were thousands, around
ten thousand people, who came to listen to the message. We
hope to baptize these people in the near future."[63]

On August 28, 1966, the "Rombongan Evangelisasi Massal
DGI Wilajah Sumatra" (Mass Evangelization Group of the
Sumatra Section, Indonesian Council of Churches), numbering about a thousand persons, visited Tandjung Lankat. On
September 23, a similar group numbering seven-hundred-
fifty persons visited Namo Ukur, and later other groups visited
a total of twenty-nine villages during 1966. These evangelization meetings were attended not only by Karo Bataks but
also by large numbers of Javanese plantation workers living
in North Sumatra. One HKBP congregation in Medan has
baptized over a thousand Javanese in the last year.

---

62 Grothaus, *op. cit.*, pp. 4ff.
63 Asal Simandjuntak, Letter of July 14, 1966.

The mass evangelization teams visited thirteen more villages in 1967, and continue to organize evangelization to villages on invitation. They report problems in managing the large evangelization teams, covering the wide areas of Deli-Serdang, financing the expeditions, securing enough literature and evangelization materials, and finding qualified Bible teachers.

A follow-up team from the Sumatra DGI Regional Office was assigned to each village where the mass evangelization took place. Two follow-up programs have been carried out. The first one, from July to August, 1966, included four pendeta from the HKBP, three pendeta from the GBKP, one from the HKI, and two religious teachers. A second program from September through October, 1966, included fourteen HKBP pendeta, four pendeta and elders from the GBKP, and two religious teachers from the HKI. The Indonesian Christian Student Movement, a branch of the SCM, has also assisted the evangelization teams, and there have been short courses for laymen who will be going into the Karo area to work as teachers in the congregations. On the east coast interchurch committees of pendeta and laymen have been formed in several areas to coordinate activities. The visitation of villages and prebaptismal instruction are carried out by congregational teachers and other laymen. The Karo pendeta are so few that they can do little more than supervise. Theological professors and seminary students have also helped in baptismal instruction during the summer months, and all of the churches have contributed personnel. Wherever qualified teachers, who could also speak Karo Batak, were found, the program has progressed most effectively. The Karo Bataks prefer to study Christianity in their own dialect. Elsewhere the program of evangelization has relied on interpreters.

The GBKP has added more than forty thousand new baptized members since 1966, bringing the total present membership to about seventy-five thousand including children, with about fifteen thousand more taking catechetical instruction in preparation for baptism.[64] The HKBP expects to send

---

[64] Laporan Panita Evangelisasi Massal, DGI Wilajah Sumatra Untuk

pendeta and laymen into the area for several years until
more Karo students graduate from seminary. Seldom have
"Lutheran" churches been so zealous to secure members for
a neighboring "Reformed" sister church.

There is great concern among the Christians of North Sumatra to understand the meaning of this sudden attraction
to Christianity. Some credit the long history of missionary
work among the Karo. Others point to the recurrent theme
of mass movement among the Bataks. Still others credit a
disenchantment with the Communist program, or government
pressure for the Karo to join Christianity or Islam. "The
urging of the state can be dangerous to the Church and
holds little promise if the police or soldiers go into a village
and demand that the people decide, displaying lists of those
who decided. In this way many Karo have entered baptismal
instruction."[65] However, the number of converts is highest
in the areas of the Karo highlands where the government
has not exerted pressure. "It can be stated that in villages
the number of baptismal applicants climbs primarily through
the intensified missionary activity of the local congregation."[66]
The complicated phenomenon of mass conversion has always
escaped any simple explanation. The mass movement to
Christianity is not a simple reaction to the insecurity of
political chaos nor a sudden appreciation for values of social
justice in the church that might be especially appropriate
under the new political regime. The Batak Christians are
most concerned because they are not quite sure why the mass
conversion of Karo Bataks has progressed with such intensity
at this particular time.

The anthropologist Alan Tippett suggests that we under-

Daerah Karo, Sidang Lengkap I, DGI Wilajah Sumatra, Berastagi, June
5-9, 1967.

[65] Grothaus, *op. cit.*, pp. 5ff.

[66] *Ibid.* For a description of Batak village life at this time see Masri
Singarimbun, "Kutagamber: A Village of the Karo," pp. 115-28 in
Koentjaraningrat, *Villages in Indonesia* (Cornell University Press, Ithaca,
N.Y., 1967). For a description of the mass evangelization by an eye-
witness see Elizabeth Goldsmith, *Batak Miracle* (London: Overseas Mis-
sionary Fellowship, 1967).

stand rapid growth in Batak churches during periods of crisis as the climax of gradual development from multiple causes. Individuals witnessed that under Christianity the family structure did not disintegrate, Christians valued the adat and organization of local society, enhancing rather than impairing the group welfare, and that Christianity was a religious orientation to life. This general understanding nurtured a growing belief that the new orientation of Christianity might be more adequate to cope with crises in modern society. Speaking of the Bataks, Tippett maintains that "individual conviction of the rightness of Christianity does not usually bring much action until some socially cohesive entity has built up a 'reservoir of tension' that reaches a breaking point, at which point the whole flood comes at once."[67]

The most probable explanation is that the rapid church growth is part of a pattern in Karo Batak society. The rapid social and economic changes which have swept through Karoland in recent years are demanding a new belief and value orientation from the Bataks. Until recent years the Karo economy has been static and generally unproductive. With modernization the Karo Batak's pattern of economic behavior has changed substantially, resulting in a highly productive economy. Accelerated economic growth particularly in the last few years is documented by several independent field surveys and research studies carried out through the University of North Sumatra. These studies describe the recent economic performance of the Karo as especially "development-minded," motivated to increase their income and able to take advantage of economic opportunities.[68] Changes in the value system may then be a direct result of changes in the social and economic environment where the values and

67 Alan R. Tippett, Lecture Notes on the Batak Church: A Case Study, School of World Mission and Institute of Church Growth, Fuller Theological Seminary, Pasadena, California, 1965-1966.

68 David Penny and Masri Singarimbun, "Economic Activity Among the Karo Batak of Indonesia: A Case Study in Economic Change," *Bulletin of Indonesian Economic Studies*, No. 6, February, 1967, Department of Economics Research, School of Pacific Studies, Australian National University, Canberra, p. 39.

attitudes of Christianity appeared more attractive than either the traditional beliefs or Islam.

The pattern of rapid conversion in recent years among the Karo Bataks might then be viewed as parallel to the same recurrent phenomena of rapid church growth in other Batak tribal groups. If we compare the Karo with the Toba Bataks we find a similar social structure, adat, family system and entrepreneurial attitude. With these socio-cultural similarities we might also expect a similar response to economic development, although the developmental changes occurred somewhat later in Karoland.

Many missionary organizations are active among the Karo. The Catholics provide one of the best schools in the area for about a thousand Karo youth and are heavily subsidizing their own evangelistic activities. The Adventists have also recently erected a high school and attract many Karo. Islam as well has made headway and even allows Karo converts to eat pork if they will become Muslim. The GBKP with its thirty thousand members was not equipped to compete for the estimated four-hundred-fifty thousand Karo seeking a new way of life. At the present rate there is one applicant for baptism for every two existing members in the GBKP! The neighboring churches are themselves in financial difficulty and, while they can provide limited personnel to assist in baptismal instruction, are severely limited in the help they can give. Christian literature is in especially short supply, and the applicants for baptism "have mostly only some copied hymns, the Ten Commandments, Creed and Lord's Prayer as their 'iron ration.' When the turmoil started there were only a few small hymnals with 162 hymns available, a translation of *104 Bible Stories* and some Old and New Testaments, which were quickly sold out."[69] Funds are also needed to finance the hospital and institutional work established by former missionaries, which must be neglected as the GBKP gives its immediate attention to the new converts.

---

[69] Werner Grothaus, "Ein Volk im Aufbruch auf den guten Weg," *Welt* (April, 1967), pp. 3ff.

7. CONCLUSION

The ongoing activity of missions has survived the transition from mission field to independent churches in North Sumatra. Each church, responding to the stimulus of foreign missions, has borrowed from local tradition as well as Westernized innovation to produce a unique combination. Some elements were accepted, others were modified, while still others were rejected outright. The process of differentiation is still blurred in its accelerated adaptation to the political, economic, and social situation in modern Indonesia.

This study, in describing the transitional stages leading to independent Batak churches, seeks to provide a basis for estimating foreign missionary activity in North Sumatra, understanding the rapid changes currently taking place and anticipating problems of other younger churches. The multiplicity of missionary organizations and churches working among the Batak people has given us the opportunity to compare a variety of approaches and consequent results. The rapid expansion of the RMG contrasts with the more cautious Methodist advancement. The dependence on government subsidy, private enterprise, or local contributions to supplement mission funds also differentiates the missionary-sending groups. Each group was active in institutional work, with schools being the most important source of new members, closely followed by medical services. The original boundaries of comity, established by the Dutch, were not able to withstand the pressures of modernization and cultural integration. Although many of the more recent missionary-sending groups undoubtedly secured members from the established Christian community, there was a remarkable degree of harmony between the foreign missionary organizations. The denominational alignment of RMG-sponsored churches has not destroyed regional ecumenicity, as anticipated by some when the HKBP joined the LWF. Whether the Christian community will ultimately unite across ethnic and denominational boundaries or will divide itself according to either ethnic lines or the denominational affiliation of their origin is not yet certain. In any case, the responsibility to assist

Batak churches has not yet been fulfilled by the foreign Christian community.

Batak society has been marked by a fascination with change itself in the process of modernization. In traditional society change was a heresy severely regulated and restrained. In the New Order the inflated influence of youth and students and the millennial hope for a better future have combined with a rejection of the past and dissatisfaction with the present. In its orientation to the future, Christianity has a particular attraction to those in a context of unrestrained change. While the past traditions grow increasingly distant, the future continues to be remote and uncertain, lending a sense of immediacy to the present. The Batak churches will have a difficult time adjusting to modern Indonesian society while retaining their roots in traditions of Batak society and culture.

None of the younger churches is "typical" in the sense that they all follow a unilinear pattern of development. The Batak churches have, however, been among the first products of nineteenth-century mission activity to emerge from the mission field. As these Batak churches establish their own mission fields in neighboring areas, familiar problems are certain to arise. Ecumenical cooperation with sister churches, although not necessarily organizational merger, has proven itself essential to fulfill their mutual responsibility for church and nation. The Batak churches dare not define their responsibility according to either tribal or denominational boundaries, but must extend Christian service and witness across tribal, denominational, and national borders. Religion carries a great responsibility for the integration, legitimation, and implementation of authority in countries such as modern Indonesia.

In tracing the history of Batak churches it is more important to ask the right questions than supply simplistic solutions to the problems of Christianity incarnated in Batakland. The differentiated complexity of Batak church life defies any simple explanation or causal hypothesis. As elsewhere in Indonesia, there is considerable mystery and mystique associated with religion in Batakland.

BIBLIOGRAPHY

The following references, while not of equal importance or reliability, contributed to the opinions expressed in the foregoing book. This list of references does not include all sources cited in the footnotes, omitting several primary sources or other titles either of less importance or such scarce supply as to be generally unobtainable. Other standard references on the Bataks are omitted as well, but can be located in Gerald Anderson's bibliographical guide on Christianity in Southeast Asia.

Anderson, Gerald H., ed. *Christianity in Southeast Asia.* New Haven, Conn.: The Missionary Research Library and Yale University Southeast Asian Studies, 1966.

Bartlett, H. H., "A Batak and Malay Chant on Rice Cultivation, with Introductory Notes on Bilingualism and Acculturation in Indonesia," *Proceedings of the American Philosophical Society,* XCVI (1952).

———, "The Labors of the Datoe," *Papers of the Michigan Academy of Science, Arts and Letters, 1929-1930.* Ann Arbor, Mich.: University of Michigan, 1930.

———,"The Symbolic Grave-Post (Anisan) of the Batak of Asahan," *Papers of the Michigan Academy of Science, Arts and Letters.* New York: Macmillan, 1923.

Bendtz, N. Arne, "Faith of the Batak," *Frontiers,* XII, 5 (January, 1961).

———, "Lutheran Strategies in World Mission," *Augustana Theological Seminary Review,* IX, 2 (1957).

Beyerhaus, Peter, and H. Lefever. *The Responsible Church and the Foreign Mission.* Grand Rapids: Eerdmans, 1964.

Bridston, Keith, "A Younger Church in Stormy Seas," *Lutheran World,* II (Spring, 1955).

Bruner, Edward M., and Alan O. Ross, "Family Interaction at Two Levels of Acculturation in Sumatra," *American Journal of Orthopsychiatry,* XXXIII, 5 (October, 1963).

Bruner, Edward M., "Kinship Organization Among the Batak of Sumatra," pp. 118-125 of *Transactions of the New York Academy of Sciences,* Series II, Vol. XXII, No. 1 (November, 1959).

———, "The Toba Batak Village," pp. 52-64 in William G. Skinner, *Local, Ethnic, and National Loyalties in Village Indonesia.* New Haven, Conn.: Yale University Cultural Report Series, 1959.

———, "Urbanization and Ethnic Identity in North Sumatra," pp. 508-521 in *American Anthropologist,* LXIII (1961).

———, "Medan, The Role of Kinship in an Indonesian City," in Alexander

Spoehr, ed. *Pacific Port Towns and Cities: A Symposium,* held at the Tenth Pacific Science Congress, Honolulu, Hawaii, 1961. Honolulu: Bishop Museum Press, 1963.

Burton, Richard, and Nathaniel Ward, "Report of a Journey into Batak Country in the Year 1824," *Transactions of the Royal Asiatic Society,* Vol. I. London, 1827.

Cunningham, Clark E. *The Postwar Migration of the Toba-Bataks to East Sumatra.* New Haven, Conn.: Yale University Cultural Report Series, 1958.

Davis, Merle. *The Economic Basis of the Church.* Tambaram Madras Series, Vol. V. London: Oxford, 1939.

de Kleine, H. F. *Christ Is the Victor.* Trans. William G. Reitzer. Wuppertal-Barmen: Verlag der Rheinischen/Missionsgesellschaft, 1952.

Dewaard, Nellie. *Pioneer in Sumatra.* London: China Inland Mission, 1962.

Ellwanger, Joseph, "The Batak Protestant Christian Church," *Concordia Theological Monthly,* XXX, 1 (January, 1959).

Freytag, Walter. *Spiritual Revolution in the East.* Trans. L. M. Stalker. London: Lutterworth, 1940.

Goldsmith, Elizabeth. *Batak Miracle.* London: Overseas Missionary Fellowship, 1967.

Gonda, Dr. J. *Sanskrit in Indonesia.* Nagpur, India: International Academy of Indian Culture, 1952.

Gould, James W. *Americans in Sumatra.* The Hague: Martinus Nijhoff, 1961.

Grothaus, Werner, "Ein Volk im Aufbruch auf den guten Weg," *Welt,* March and April, 1967.

Heine-Geldern, Robert von, "Prehistoric Research in the Netherlands Indies," pp. 129-167 in *Science and Scientists in the Netherlands Indies.* Eds. Pieter Honig and Frans Verdorn. New York; Cambridge, Mass.: Riverside, 1945.

Hemmers, J. H., "Sketches from the Life of Nommensen, The Apostle to the Bataks" (trans. R. L. Archer), *The Malaysia Message,* from XLV, 9 (September, 1935) to XLIX, 10 (October, 1939).

Huria Kristen Batak Protestant. *Seratus Tahun Kekristenan Dalam Sedjarah Rakjat Batak.* Tarutung, 1961.

Keuning, Johannes. *The Toba Batak, Formerly and Now.* Ithaca: Cornell University Modern Indonesia Project, 1958.

Kraemer, Hendrik. *From Mission Field to Independent Church.* London: SCM, 1958.

Lehman. *Gottes Volk im vielen Ländern.* Berlin: Evangelische Verlagsanstalt, 1955.

Loeb, Edwin M. *Sumatra, Its History and People.* Vienna: Verlag des Institutes für Völkerkunde, der Universität, Wien, 1935.

Low, James, "An Account of the Batta Race in Sumatra," *The Journal of the Royal Asiatic Society of Great Britain and Ireland,* Vol. II. London, 1835.

Lumbantobing, Andar, "Christian Education in the Batak Church," *Lutheran World*, II (Autumn, 1955).

―――, "Sahala of a Medicine Man and a Theological Graduate," *South East Asian Journal of Theology*, January, 1963.

―――, "The Confession of the Batak Church," in Vilmos Vajta and Hans Weissgerber. *The Church and the Confessions*. Philadelphia: Fortress, 1963.

Marsden, William. *The History of Sumatra*. London: J. McCreery, 1811.

Müller-Krüger, Th. *Sedjarah Geredja di Indonesia*. Djakarta: Badan Penerbit Kristen, 1959.

Needham, Hester. *God First: Hester Needham's Work in Sumatra*. Ed. Mary Enfield. London: Religious Tract Society, 1898.

Peltzer, Karl J., "Western Impact on East Sumatra and North Tapanuli," *Journal of South East Asia History*, II, 2 (1961).

Rauws, Johannes, H. Kraemer, F. J. F. van Hasselt, and N. A. C. Slatemaker de Bruine. *The Netherlands Indies*. World Dominion, 1935.

Rheinischen Missionsgesellschaft. *Gemacht zu seinem Volk*. Wuppertal-Barmen: Verlag der RMG, 1962.

Ross, Alan O., "Ego Identity and the Social Order: A Psychosocial Analysis of Six Indonesians," *Psychological Monographs*, Vol. LXXVI, No. 23, No. 542, 1962.

Sarumpaet-Hutabarat, Julia, "Women Under the Adat," *Lutheran World*, II (Summer, 1955).

Scherer, James Arnold. "The Development of a Lutheran Missionary Tradition and Its Relation to the Ecumenical Movement." Ph.D. dissertation, Union Theological Seminary, New York, 1967.

Schiotz, Fredrik A., "Lutheran World Missions," *International Review of Missions*, XLIII (1954).

Schreiner, Lothar. *Das Bekenntnis der Batak-Kirche*, Theologische Existenz Heute. München: Chr. Kaiser Verlag, 1966.

―――, "Hospital to Theological Seminary: Nommensen University," *Lutheran World*, V, 1 (June, 1958).

Simatupang, T. B., "Life in Christ—Called to Service and Nation-Building," in Soritua A. E. Nababan. *Christ The Life*. Dumaguette City, Philippines: Report of the Asian Christian Youth Assembly, 1965.

Simon, Gottfried. *Progress and Arrest of Islam in Sumatra*. London: Marshall Brothers, 1914.

Tahun Indjil Kristus Di Simalungun, 2 September, 1903 to September 2, 1963. Pematang Siantar: Pimpinan Pusat, GKPS, 1963.

Tobing, Philip, "Dr. Nommensen and the Rapid Christianization and Development of North Tapanuli in Sumatra," *De Heerbaan*, September 10, 1964.

―――. *The Structure of the Toba Batak Belief in the High God*. Amsterdam: Jacob van Campen, 1956.

Van der Kroef, Justus M., "Messianic Movements in the Celebes, Sumatra and Borneo," in Sylvia L. Thrupp. *Millennial Dreams in Action*. The Hague: Mouton, 1962.

Vergouwen, J. C. *The Social Organization and Customary Law of the Toba Batak of Northern Sumatra.* Trans. Jeune Scott-Kemball. The Hague: Martinus Nijhoff, 1964.

Verwiebe, E., "Youth Problem in the Batak Church in Sumatra," *International Review of Missions,* April, 1938.

Wales, H. G. Quaritch, "The Cosmological Aspect of Indonesian Religion," *Journal of the Royal Asiatic Society,* London, 1959.

Warneck, Johannes, "The Growth of the Church in the Mission Field," *International Review of Missions,* I, 1 (1912).

———. *The Living Christ and Dying Heathenism.* London: Revell, 1909.

PROTESTANT CHURCH ORGANIZATIONS IN NORTH SUMATRA REGISTERED WITH THE DEPARTMENT OF RELIGION

1. Huria Kristen Batak Protestant (Pearadja, Tarutung)
2. Geredja Kristen Protestant Simalungun (Dj.Djdrl. Sudirman 24, P.Siantar)
3. Geredja Kristen Batak (Dj. Sutomo 24, P.Siantar)
4. Huria Kristen Indonesia (Dj. Marihat 109, P.Siantar)
5. Geredja Batak Karo Protestant (Kabandjahe)
6. Methodist Indonesia (Dj. Hang Tuah, Medan)
7. Geredja Pentakosta (Dj. Lingga 24, P.Siantar)
8. Geredja Pentakosta Indonesia (Dj. Singamangaradja 9, P.Siantar)
9. Mission Batak (Dj. Abdullah Lubis 65, Medan)
10. Pentakosta (Pd. K.Siburian) (Dj. Asahan 35, P.Siantar)
11. Geredja Pantekosta di Indonesia (Dj. Pd. Bulan 261, Medan)
12. Balai Keselamatan (Dj.Samanhudi 27, Medan)
13. Geredja Protestant Indonesia Bhagian Barat (Dj. Diponegoro 27, Medan)
14. Gereformerd (Dj. Palang Merah 112, Medan)
15. Masehi Advent Hari Ketudjuh (Dj.Simbolon 6, P.Siantar)
16. Masehi Advent Conference (Belakang PON. Medan)
17. Sidang Demaat Allah (Dj. Iskandar Muda, Medan)
18. Geredja Merdeka Protestant Indonesia (Dj.Hajam Wuruk 40, Medan)
19. Geredja Pantekosta Serikat Indonesia (Dj. Purnamajati 31, Medan)
20. The Christian Church (no address)
21. Geredja Bethel Tabernakel (Dj. Mergat 2c, Medan)
22. Pantekosta/Pinksterkerk (Dj. Tomat 6b, Medan)
23. Geredja Bethel Indjil Sepenuh (Dj. S.K.I. Aeknauli Tromol Pos 34, P.Siantar)
24. Masehi Pentakosta Damai Bunuraja Baru (d/p Kepala Bhagian Kristen Kabandjahe)
25. Sidang Roholkudus (Dj. Sei.Wampu 56, Medan)

26. Geredja Kerasulan Baru (Kebun Limau Mungkur Tandjung Morawa)
27. Geredja Masehi Indjil Sangihi/Talaud (Dj.Sei Bentu 1, Medan)
28. Huria Hatopan ni Kristus Jesus (P.Djorlang Hataran Kp. Hutadipar, T. Balata, P.Siantar)
29. Pantekosta Maranatha (no address)
30. Geredja Methodist Merdeka Indonesia (Dj.Ps.Merah 22, Medan)
31. Geredja Kristen Protestant Indonesia (Dj.Dr.Tjipto 40, P. Siantar)
32. Geredja Kristen Kalam Kudus (Dj.Bali 34, Medan)
33. The Indonesian Baptist Mission (Dj. Ir.H.Djuanda 7, Medan)
34. Kemah Indjil Geredja Masehi Indonesia (Dj.Thamrin 42, Tebing Tinggi)
35. Geredja Pentakosta Sumatra Utara (Balige, Sumatra Utara)
36. Mennonit (Padang Sidempuan)
37. Punguan Kristen Batak (Padang Sidempuan)
38. Huria Kristen Protestant Baru (Hutahajan, Laguboti)
39. HKBP. Luther (Lumban Siagian, Tarutung)
40. Pentakosta (Pd. A. Sinaga) (Dj. Marihat 78c, P.Siantar)

Kepala Djawatan Agama Kristen, Propensi Sumatra Utara,
Kepala Bhagian Urusan Agama, Medan.

THE TOTAL NUMBER OF PROTESTANT
CHRISTIANS IN BATAKLAND, OCTOBER 12, 1968

SUMATRA TIMUR (EAST SUMATRA)	1,222,550
TAPANULI	1,034,200
TOTAL	2,256,750
THE TOTAL NUMBER OF ROMAN CATHOLICS	200,000
GRAND TOTAL	2,456,750

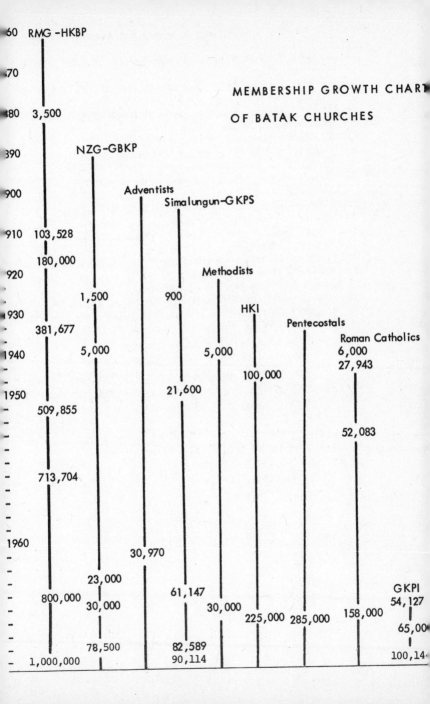

MEMBERSHIP GROWTH CHART
OF BATAK CHURCHES

INDEX OF PEOPLE, PLACES,
AND ORGANIZATIONS

279.1
P37

36009

622-1
5-39

3 4711 00228 6922

LINCOLN CHRISTIAN COLLEGE